MW00780061

The War in Florida
by
Woodburne Potter

Enhanced Edition
with Introduction, Endnotes, and Index by
John & Mary Lou Missall

Seminole Wars Foundation, Inc.
Dade City, FL

The Seminole Wars Foundation, Inc.
35427 Reynolds St.
Dade City, FL 33523

www.seminolewars.us

ISBN: 978-0-9821105-3-9

Cover painting ". . . From Right, Left and Centre"
by Jackson Walker, www.jacksonwalkerstudio.com

Contents

Maps of Dade's Battle and Camp Izard can be found between pages 138-139.

The Seminole Wars Foundation

The Seminole Wars Foundation, Inc. was founded in 1992 with the goal of preserving sites significant to the Seminole Wars, establishing educational programs to disseminate information about the wars, and to publish books and other matter pertaining to these important but little understood conflicts.

The Foundation has been instrumental in the preservation of the Camp Izard battle site, has purchased portions of the Fort Dade site and funded excavations upon it, and has assisted in the purchase and preservation of the Fort King site in Ocala. Foundation members have given numerous talks to civic organizations, student groups, and the general public.

For further information contact the Seminole Wars Foundation at 352-583-2711, by mail at 35247 Reynolds St., Dade City, FL 33523, or visit our website at www.seminolewars.us.

A list of our publications can be found on page 185.

Introduction

For those who wish to study first-hand accounts of the Second Seminole War, there are a handful of books that are required reading. The first, of course, is John Sprague's *The Florida War*, followed by Jacob Motte's *Journey into Wilderness*, John Bemrose's *Reminiscences*, Henry Prince's diary, and a few others. One of the most important of these accounts is Woodburne Potter's *The War in Florida*, first published in 1836. Although Potter was only in Florida for a few months of what would turn out to be a seven-year conflict, he was present at a critical time, and, as personal secretary to one of the army's most senior officers, was privy to information that others might lack. He was also a keen observer of details, dedicated to understanding the causes of the conflict, and not the least bit hesitant to give his opinion of it all.

The Second Seminole War was part of the much larger problem of how to reconcile the wants of the rapidly growing American nation with the rights of those aboriginal nations who had lived here for centuries. The solution decided upon by President Andrew Jackson and Congress was to remove all Native American nations from the eastern portion of the country and resettle them out west. Caught up in this effort were the Seminole Indians who resided in what was then the largely unsettled Florida Territory. As government pressure on them increased, Seminole resolve to remain in their homeland only became stronger.

Tensions increased until December of 1835, when war seemed to explode upon the Territory. On the 28th, a column of 108 soldiers under the command of Maj. Francis L. Dade was virtually wiped out as it passed through the Seminole heartland. A few days later, a force of about 750 men under Brig. Gen. Duncan Clinch was repulsed at the Withlacoochee

River. All across the peninsula, isolated homesteads and prosperous plantations were attacked, torched, and their occupants murdered or forced to flee for their lives. Florida, it seemed, was in flames.

News of the outbreak travelled as swiftly as it could in those days, yet it still took about two weeks to reach New Orleans, where Maj. Gen. Edmund P. Gaines was on an inspection tour. Gaines was head of the Western Department of the United States Army, and most of the fighting in Florida had taken place within his jurisdiction. Although trouble was brewing on the border with Mexico (the Texas Rebellion) Gaines felt compelled to act. He couldn't wait for orders, which might take weeks to arrive from Washington. After gathering what federal troops were available in the area and calling on the State of Louisiana for volunteers, Gaines set sail for Florida on February 4, 1836 and arrived at Tampa Bay five days later. With him was his personal aide, Woodburne Potter.

Very little is known about Potter, not even how old he was when he came to Florida. Surprisingly, we cannot state with 100% certainty that he even wrote the book. Authorship is given as being "By a Late Staff Officer" who is unnamed. Yet even that statement appears to be inaccurate. His scant military record lists him as receiving his 2nd Lieutenant's commission on August 16, 1837, well over a year after he left Florida. The fact is backed up by a letter from General Gaines to the Secretary of War dated April 1837, personally recommending Potter for the Commission. In truth, Potter appears to have been a civilian working for General Gaines, a position he had held since at least 1833, when he is mentioned as a clerk to the general on an aqueduct project. On page 148 Potter lists the wounded on the first day of battle at Camp Izard. Among them is "Mr. W. Potter, secretary to the General." The other wounded personnel are listed with their military ranks.[1]

Potter's actual military career lasted about two years. For most of that time he served as aide-de-camp to General Gaines, as evidenced by several letters he signed on behalf of

vi

Gaines bearing his name and title. Something may have happened in late 1837 to remove him from the position. The post returns for March 1839 for Fort Brooke at Tampa Bay list him as being "absent, without leave" since November of 1838. Potter would resign his commission in August of 1839.[2]

Potter's paper trail after leaving the army is almost non-existent. He may have returned to his home state of Pennsylvania. Mention is made of a Woodburne Potter living in Washington, DC, in 1846 and working as a lobbyist for the Philadelphia Naval Shipyard. Whether or not it is the same person is unknown, though his connections to the military establishment would have proved useful in such a position. If we assume he did take up residence in Philadelphia, then we find a Woodburne Potter being buried on May 27, 1847 in a $50 flannel-lined black coffin with engraved plate and two rows of moldings. Beyond that, the trail is cold.[3]

Although Potter's book is valuable as a record of events that happened during the first few months of the war, it is perhaps more valuable for what it says about the causes of the war. After two short chapters describing Florida and the Seminoles, he spends nearly half of the remainder of the book examining what led up to the conflict. In this he is most refreshing, not buying into the official explanation that blamed everything on the Indians. Indeed, as far as Potter was concerned, nearly all the responsibility rested either in Washington or with unscrupulous Florida residents. At the same time, he was not above placing part of the blame on Seminoles who were either too eager for war or not willing to accept what Potter saw as inevitable.

At the same time, the reader must remember that Potter was a man of his own times. He didn't seem to have any problem with the Seminoles being encouraged to give up their homes and move west. Like most Americans of the time, his attitude toward the Indians was paternal. The "Great Father, the President" knew what was best for the "children of the forest." What he did have a problem with is the manner in which the removal was accomplished. Everywhere he looked, he saw lying, stealing, and cheating on the part of the whites. He also saw bungling and inefficiency within the army. As far as he was concerned, the whole ghastly experience could have been prevented if everyone, including the Seminoles, had done what they were supposed to.

Potter was in Florida for only two or three months, and much of the information he gives is second-hand. His details about events preceding the war and those concerning Dade's and Clinch's battles seem to be derived from interviews with people who were there or had spoken to someone who was there. Likewise, his accounts of General Winfield Scott's campaign, which took place soon after General Gaines departed the Territory, were most likely gleaned from letters, various reports, or conversations with veterans of the campaign. By his own admission, Potter was in Florida at the time of Scott's campaign, convalescing from wounds received at Camp Izard. This would have given him ample opportunity to speak with people who had been on the campaign and perhaps read official reports. Thus, while this at first seems to be a primary source, much of it must be taken at less than face value. We must also remember that as an aide to Gaines, he was inclined to be biased in that man's favor.

Soon after Gaines's army of over a thousand men arrived at Tampa Bay on February 9, 1836, they set out on the military trail that led to Fort King, located near what would later be the city of Ocala. It was a simple dirt road that went through the heart of the Seminole territory. About halfway along their trek, they came upon the remains of the slaughtered command of Major Dade. No white man had been there for over six weeks. After burying the 106 bodies, they continued on to Fort King, where they expected provisions to be waiting. Unfortunately, those supplies had yet to arrive. Short on food, Gaines decided to return to Tampa Bay. This time he would take a route that would lead him to the wetlands near the Withlacoochee River, a place where it was believed the Seminoles had gathered.

Gaines and his men reached the Withlacoochee on February 27, only to find the Seminoles waiting on the other side and determined not to let the army cross. Equally determined not to retreat, Gaines dug in and erected Camp Izard. For over a week, the army and the Seminoles skirmished, and it was here that Potter received his wounds. Running out of food and reduced to eating their horses, Gaines called on General Clinch for relief. Unable to attack the Seminoles in their strongholds south of the river, Gaines and his men retreated north to Fort Drane, located on Clinch's plantation. Having received orders to proceed to the Texas frontier, Gaines departed Florida a few days later, leaving the convalescent Potter behind, where he began the research that led to this book.

Notes on the Enhanced Edition

In publishing this new edition of *The War in Florida*, the Seminole Wars Foundation decided to improve upon what was already a valuable book. Although the work had been out of print for quite awhile, in recent years facsimile editions have been easy to come by. One problem with the original and facsimile editions is that they lack many of the things modern-day scholars have come to rely on. Most important, because Potter didn't make an index, the newer editions rarely have one. Potter lists an amazing number of names for such a small volume, many of which would otherwise be lost to history and difficult to find without an index. We also felt the book needed endnotes in addition to Potter's footnotes. People and places perhaps generally known at the time but now obscure need to be identified or information about them clarified.

In some cases, Potter may have been using information that we now know is in error. Historians have learned much more about the war than was known at the time, and we felt this knowledge should be passed on to the reader. Indeed, this became one of the most difficult parts of the editing process. Should we point out every little error? To do so might make certain passages unreadable because of all the bracketed comments. In the end, we felt it was best to point out the most important errors and warn readers not to take Potter's reports as absolute fact, especially for situations where he was not present.

Facsimile editions are little more than photographic reproductions of the original edition. In order to add endnotes and the occasional editorial comment, it was necessary to re-type the entire document. This introduces a problem: Because of differences in typeface, font size, page size, and margins, the page numbers would not come out the same. This, in turn, poses a problem for anyone who is looking up something another author referred to in Potter's book. If a citation is said to be on page 137 of Potter's original edition, then it needs to be on page 137 of *all* editions of the book, including this one.

To resolve this issue, each page was broken in the same place as the original. Unfortunately, this does not produce a perfect result, and the reader will notice that very often the bottom line on a page does not extend all the way to the right margin. More annoyingly, the last line usually does not reach the bottom of the page. We attempted to minimize this by moving hyphenated or inconsequential words to or from the subsequent page, but could not completely eliminate the problem. Most of the pages were inexplicably short until we discovered that in Potter's original, the printer had changed line spacing after page 176, thereby putting more lines on each page. To make the book more pleasing to the eye, we followed his example. In the end, we felt these compromises were a small price to pay to keep the book consistent with earlier editions.

Another issue that resulted from creating a new document was the matter of typographical errors in the text. In a facsimile, there is no question as to who made the mistake; you're seeing it as it was originally published. In something that is re-typed, the reader can't be sure where the error originated. We would never be so bold as to say we've introduced no errors, but we have closely compared our work to the original to make sure that Potter's text is the same in both versions, errors and all.

Still, there are idiosyncrasies in the original text that the reader might think are errors. The most obvious is spelling. Mr. Webster's dictionary was still a new thing at the time, and education in America was far from standardized. For the most part, Potter's spelling is good, but he used what we would consider "British" spelling, such as colour, neighbour, centre, lustre, practise, authorised, and defence. Words that the reader will easily recognize as such are not marked with a [*sic*].

Another problem with spelling arises when it comes to names, especially Indian names. In one paragraph (page 20), the same Indian's name is spelled three different ways. When a person or place name has a different spelling than what is common today, we usually placed it in brackets after Potter's entry. The most obvious is Osceola, which Potter gives as Assiola. Grammar was also inconsistent at the time, especially when it came to capitalization. While most of the time his capitalization rules are not too different from today's, the one notable exception is "river" following the name of a river, as in Ouithlacoochee river. We also felt it necessary to retain Potter's italics, small capitals, and other stylistic preferences.

To avoid any confusion, footnotes in the text are Potter's originals; endnotes are our additions. Likewise, anything in brackets are insertions by the editors. In the few instances when Potter used brackets (pages 62, 66 & 156), we changed those to parentheses for clarity. In the one editorial comment that Potter put "ed." in, we changed it to "W. P." to eliminate confusion (page 62).

The reader will also note that the page headers in the final chapter change from "Commencement of Hostilities" to "The War" after a few pages, but there is no new chapter. That is how it is in the original, and we preserved it that way. Overall, one gets the impression the original book was rushed to press without adequate proofreading.

A number of individuals he mentions left no historical trace or could not be positively identified and are therefore not mentioned in the endnotes. For many of the state volunteer officers, only a first name or initial could be found. In these instances we simply put that information in brackets before the surname instead of having the reader refer to an endnote to see what the man's first name was. The source for those names is given at the beginning of the endnotes.

The Seminole Wars Foundation hopes you enjoy this new edition and that our enhancements help in your understanding of this tragic and largely forgotten conflict.

THE

WAR

IN

FLORIDA:

BEING

AN EXPOSITION OF ITS CAUSES,

AND

AN ACCURATE HISTORY

OF THE

CAMPAIGNS

OF

GENERALS

CLINCH, GAINES AND SCOTT.

"ON THIS SUBJECT MANY PERSONS HAVE SAID MUCH, EVERY BODY SOMETHING, AND
NO MAN ENOUGH."

BY A LATE STAFF OFFICER.

BALTIMORE:

LEWIS AND COLEMAN.

1836.

TO

THE HON. COLONEL

JOSEPH M. WHITE, M. C.

BRIGADIER GENERAL

DUNCAN L. CLINCH, U. S. A.

AND

THE HON. COLONEL

JAMES GADSDEN:

Names identified with the interest and prosperity of Florida,

this History is most respectfully dedicated,

BY THEIR FRIEND

AND SERVANT,

THE AUTHOR.

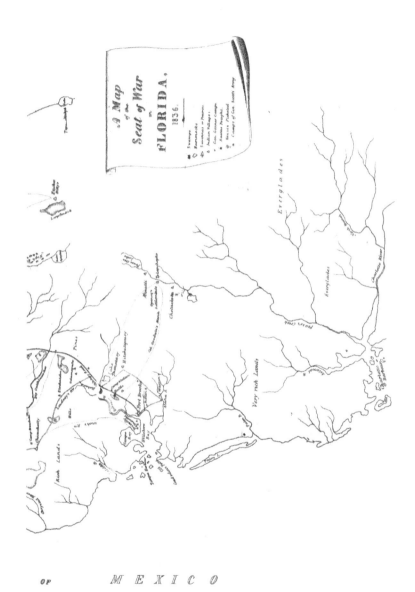

A Map
of the
Seat of War
in
FLORIDA,
1836.

Swamps.
Hammocks.
Townships or Prairies.
Indian Villages.
Gen. Gaines' Camps.
Gen. Scott's Camps.
Inactive Dragoons.
Houses (Probable)
Camps of Gen. Scott's Army.

Everglades

Everglades

Very rich Lands

G U L F   O F   M E X I C O

xix

TO THE PUBLIC.

WHEN the author of the following pages joined the Army, which hastened to the rescue of the suffering inhabitants of Florida, he was led, by his invariable custom when abroad, to take notes of passing events. The campaign ending, and himself having been detained several weeks in the peninsula by the result of a slight wound which he received at Camp Izard,[4] he discovered the great ignorance of the people as to the origin of the difficulties with the Seminoles;—this increased his anxiety to become acquainted with the facts, and especially when it was hinted that the *agents* had more or less contributed to the evil. Occasionally an intelligent, frank and communicative settler would fall in his track, from whom he reaped much valuable information—whilst a less favoured one, who chuckled in the pride of having inflicted upon the savage a brutal beating, imparted many startling incidents. Thus he was furnished with materials to prosecute an inquiry, which he forthwith commenced, and has since pursued, through personal presence, friends, offices and archives, overlooking nothing that shed the least light upon the subject,—still, with the remotest idea of ever publishing it, nor would he consent for a long time to permit the importunities of those who had perused his rough notes to swerve him from his determination.

In discussing this painfully interesting subject, he has spoken boldly and fearlessly—animadverting without restraint, and holding up the guilty to the just indignation of a suffering people—challenging a denial of the truth of his remarks, and pledging himself for the correctness of his version of the campaign. Many little incidents have necessarily been omitted in consequence of the limits of the work, but nothing that he conceives would materially enhance its interest.

The Map of the Seat of War, prepared expressly for the occasion, has been approved of by the most intelligent officers of our army who have resided in the interior of that country, and by one whose topographical knowledge of it is more extensive and accurate than that of any other individual living, and under whose special eye it was drawn.

The sketch of the massacre ground of the lamented Dade[5] and his companions, and of Camp Izard on the Ouithlacoochee [Withlacoochee], which is celebrated for the privations and distresses which its inmates patiently endured, were drawn on the spot, and are correct in every respect.

The names of the principal Chiefs and Sub-Chiefs were

furnished by a gentleman who was, until the war, intimately associated with them. The author is well aware that the English names are *not literal* translations, but their own assumed *fancy* names; as they were furnished, so he gives them. The orthography of their pronunciation in the Seminole language is correct.

In reviewing the conduct of individuals and agents of the government, he has spoken as circumstances justified. If he has been unnecessarily severe, it must not be attributed to a wilful [*sic*] disposition to misrepresent them; he belongs to *no* party—has no interests to subserve;—he aims at truth, and to expose in naked deformity the arts and machinations of those whose intrigue and deception have deluged a fair portion of our country with the blood of their fellow creatures! He has taken care not to offend, or give the least cause to the friends of the late Gen. Thompson[6] to believe that he is hostile to that estimable and much lamented man; he disavows any intention of unjust reflections, and should they unhappily exist, he sincerely regrets it.

The author does not hesitate to transfer a large share of the "glory," in producing this war in Florida, to the officers of the War Department; convinced, as he is, that if their respective duties had been properly discharged, the necessity of bloodshed would have been avoided. If the President [Andrew Jackson] was determined to gratify the craving appetites of a few avaricious speculators, it was his duty to protect the *respectable* citizens of Florida against any injury which might result from his measure; he should have thrown such a force into the territory as to prevent the possibility of a resistance; and neither can he, nor the Secretary of War,[7] stand excused in their plea of ignorance of the true state of affairs in that quarter, for they were constantly advised, not only by their agents, but by their personal friends. And it cannot be doubted, that if the Secretary of War, in replying to the call of the House of Representatives, had not *suppressed* many very important letters upon the subject, the public would not be so entirely ignorant of the *true causes of the war.* But a voluminous document (No. 271) of chaotic letters was furnished the people, which had as little bearing upon the subject, as the attempted sacrifice of General Scott[8] will have in screening General JESUP[9] *from the indignation of every honourable man in the Army!*

The difficulties which exist, and have for many years existed, on the subject of *brevet* rank[10] between the two distinguished Major Generals, will be sufficient apology for the author's abstaining from gratuitous remarks upon the conduct of either. He gives the particulars of their respective campaigns, and hazards an explanation *only* where the circumstances of the case absolutely demand it.

FLORIDA.

THIS fine territory was ceded by Spain to the United States in 1821, for spoliations committed by that nation on our commerce, estimated at 5,000,000 dollars. It is bounded on the north by Alabama and Georgia; east by the Atlantic Ocean; south by the Gulph of Mexico and Cuba channel; west by the Gulph of Mexico and the state of Alabama, from which it is divided by the river Perdido. Its shape is very irregular, extending from N. lat. 24 deg. 40 min. to 31 deg.; and from W. long. 3 deg. to 10 deg. 30 min. [ed.: Longitude at the time was measured from Washington, DC, and not Greenwich, England.] Its greatest breadth being nearly 600 miles at its northern extremity, and its mean width about 90 miles; its greatest length from north to south is 470 miles. It has an outline on the Atlantic of 550 miles, and on the north and east of the Gulph 600 miles. Its area is 55,689 square miles, or 35,635,200 acres: 15,967,360 acres of which (principally low marshy land) belong to the United States, with 4,032,640 acres of rich bottoms, which were ceded by the Seminole Indians at Payne's Landing, on the 9th of May, 1832.

Florida is divided into 15 counties, and by the census of 1830 contains 34,730 inhabitants, of whom 18,385 are whites, 15,501 are slaves, and 844 free blacks. This census however does not include the Indian population and their slaves, who are variously estimated at from 3 to 5,000. I am of opinion they will be found to have exceeded 3,700 when hostilities commenced. It is also *nominally* composed of four parts, South, West, Middle and East Florida; the latter consists of five counties—three of which have been the scenes of Indian outrage.

COUNTIES.	POPULATION.	
Duval	1970	
Nassau	1511	
	3481	
Deduct slaves	1847	= 1634
Alachua {To which hostili-}	2204	
St. John's {ties have been }	2538	
Musquito {confined. }	733	
	5475	
Deduct slaves.	2960	= 2515
White population	4149	

The upper section of Florida, from 28 deg. 34 min. to 31 deg. east and 30 deg. 35 min. to 31 deg. west, is rolling, or undulating, and moderately broken; farther south, on the peninsula, it is remarkably level and low—much of it swamps; some portions of it are similar to land supported by unsubstantial foundation, spongy, sometimes resting on alluvial matter and ometimes [*sic*] on sand. The rainy season usually sets in about the beginning of June and continues until October, when the low and level lands are inundated; these waters are drained off by the numerous lakes and small streams into the Atlantic and the Gulph of Mexico. The residue of the year but little rain falls, several weeks intervening the showers. The climate of Florida is truly delightful, and in the south, nearly tropical, the sun being quite oppressive even during the winter season; water never freezes, and frost is seldom seen south of Lake George. The summer months are very hot, the thermometer ranging from 90 deg. to 98 deg. but seldom higher; it is extremely healthy in all situations, remote from swamps and marshes, throughout the whole year. St. Augustine is the largest town in Florida, containing about 4,000 inhabitants, and the neighbouring country is a perfect Eden. The town is handsomely situated, easy of access, and from its proximity to the states presents many inducements to valetudinarians to spend the winter months there; hundreds have derived benefit from a winter residence in Florida. The country west of the Suwannee river has suffered no interruption by the Indians—their operations have been altogether confined to the east. The towns of Pensacola, Tallahassee, Appalachicola [*sic*], St. Josephs and St. Marks are progressing very rapidly, and bid fair to rival in commerce some of the northern cities; a spirit of rivalry has been generated at Appalachicola and St. Josephs which, if moderately and forbearingly carried on, is calculated to produce the most important results to both ports. From Appalachicola, lines of packet ships have been established to New York and to Liverpool. A great national naval establishment has been projected at Pensacola, and also a dry dock—funds are already at the disposal of the Executive to proceed forthwith to their completion—which, together with the rail roads and canals, will give an importance to the infant territory which, but a few years ago, it would have been esteemed madness to dream of. Much of this is owing to the indefatigable perseverance and untiring industry of their distinguished representative, Col. Joseph M. White,[11] who has also succeeded in arrangements to introduce every variety of the French, Italian and Portuguese vines, olives, vegetables, plants, &c., which are particularly suited to the climate and soil.

A large portion of the country north of 28 deg. is covered with pine forests, the trees are very tall, standing at a considerable distance apart, without underbrush, whilst the surface of the ground presents a rich carpet of verdant grass and choice flowers throughout most of the year. The alluvial bottoms and hammock lands are covered with dense forests of pine, oak, mahogany, cedar, cypress, magnolia, lob-lolly, cabbage palm, palmetto and every variety of magnificent vegetation, which frequently extends for miles, presenting one of the most imposing sights in nature. The soil of the Hammock* lands is of the most luxuriant character, and hence the desire of speculators to drive the Seminoles off, whose reserved lands are principally of this description. Adjacent to these lands you will find extensive savannas or prairies covered with tall grass, roaming through which you may count hundreds and indeed thousands of cattle; this will always render Florida a land of

---

* The Hammocks of East Florida are formed by a cluster of the richest and most redolent vegetation. The edges and interior are covered with an immense variety of small bushes, shrubs, &c., while, towering over all these, are the sweet bay, the laurel, the stately magnolia, and, indeed, every description of the most beautiful forest trees. The density of these hammocks in some places almost excludes every ray of light. Hammocks are generally found adjacent to prairie swamps, and sometimes extend, of an irregular shape, several miles.

graziers [*sic*] and of pastoral wealth. I have heard some gentlemen say they owned from 500 to 2,000 head of fine cattle that were then luxuriating in these prairies, which, if they escaped the Indian knife, would bring them from 10 to 20 dollars per head.[*] The entire coast is marked by numerous bays, bayous, lagoons, &c., whilst the interior abounds with lakes and ponds. It also possesses many curiosities, such as remarkable springs, caves, and in some places are also seen the relics of old Spanish towns, fortifications, &c.

The agricultural products of Florida have heretofore been limited, though now on the rapid increase in those parts that have escaped the desolating ravages of the Seminole. Cotton is the chief staple, of which there are three kinds cultivated,— the Mexican, green seed, and Sea-Island. Rice is also cultivated, but not to that extent it should be; it grows remarkably well on the hammock and marshy lands, and it also does well on the uplands, which produce about 70 bushels to the acre—a convincing proof that it does not require overflowed lands to make rice: the richer bottoms here give 80 or 85 bushels, and the piney lands about 60 bushels to the acre. It sells in the market towns in Florida at 75 cents per bushel, or, when cleaned, about $3.50 per 100 lbs.

The sugar cane grows finely on the good lands in Florida—3000 lbs have been produced from a single acre. But few plant the cane as yet. General Clinch[12] has perhaps the most extensive sugar plantation in the territory; he usually makes

---

[*] From a calculation made by the agent of Indian Affairs at Tallahassee, it appears that the Indians have driven off nearly 25,000 head of cattle from the neighbouring country. This estimate is founded upon the *returns* made by the owners of stock.

about 180 hogsheads of sugar, and from 70 to 80 bales of cotton, per year, together with a moderate quantity of molasses, and about 2000 bushels of corn. He also manufactures rum to a considerable extent. On this plantation is erected the picket which, in honour of Captain Drane,[13] U. S. A. is called Fort Drane.[14]

The esculent grains, generally, do not receive much attention; but corn grows admirably and large crops are made. The bene plant and palma christi are extensively cultivated and produce profitable crops. Peas, beans, pumpkins, watermelons, muskmelons, lettuce, egg plant, cucumbers, radishes, cabbage, carrots, and indeed most other vegetables are raised with ease and in great perfection.

The fig-tree flourishes excellently—two or three crops are sometimes produced a year. Oranges, limes and lemons grow in abundance: until the frost destroyed the principal groves about St. Augustine, more than a million and a half of oranges were gathered annually in that neighbourhood alone; and it is computed that, in a short time, Florida will be able to supply the demands of the whole country. All other descriptions of fruit, except those *peculiar* to northern latitudes, grow well under the genial rays of the Florida sun. The sweet potatoe is very extensively raised, even the pine barren lands are suitable to its growth. A species of the tobacco grows wild and in considerable quantities on the hammock lands.

It is somewhat remarkable, that the culture of indigo in this territory has so fallen off; at one time it was the principal export—more than one hundred and fifty thousand dollars were

6

paid in one year, in London, for Florida indigo.

The exports from the territory are cotton, sugar, cedar logs, live oak timber, boards, staves, beeswax, bricks, peltry, &c.

There are very extensive salt works on the peninsula and islands which must hereafter prove immensely profitable to the proprietors, and of vast importance to the territory.

THE SEMINOLES.

THIS tribe of Indians, whose name is indicative of their character, (the word Seminole signifying *runaway,*) are remnants of, and wanderers from, other tribes, principally of the Spanish Florida Indians, the upper Creeks or Muscogee, and the Micosukee. The latter, though but a small band, are the most relentless and ferocious of all—more bent on warring with their neighbours than pursuing the hunt. They seriously harassed General Jackson during his campaign in 1818-19,[15] and were the last to be subdued. Having burnt their villages west of the Suwannee river and made great havoc among them, he drove the remnant of their tribe to the east side of that river, when they became incorporated with the Seminoles. Their number at present does not probably exceed 400 warriors; the Creek and Spanish Indians may be estimated at 850, and the negroes at between 5 and 600—making an available force of between 1700 and 1900 warriors who have been engaged in the recent conflicts.

It may not be out of place to subjoin a list of the names of the chiefs and sub-chiefs who have been engaged in the war during the past winter, with their residences prior to the breaking out of hostilities, and their standing, or grade, in the nation at that time. What changes may have taken place since that period, of course cannot be ascertained, nor is it likely we shall ever know.

CHIEFS.	RESIDENCE.
MICONOPY,[16] Principal Chief and Governor of the Seminole nation -	Pilaklakaha[17].
JUMPER[18], Sense-keeper, and Orator of the Nation, and Chief of -	Wahoo Swamp[19].
ABRAHAM,[20] Principal Interpreter -	Pilaklaka ha [sic].
HOLATA MICO,[21] (Blue King) Principal War Chief - - - -	Ouithlocko.
YAHA HAJO,[22] (Mad Wolf) 2d Principal War Chief - - - -	Okihumky.
HITCHITI MICO, (Broken stick) 3d, &c.	Ouithlocko.
ARPIUCKI[23] (Sam Jones) 4th do. -	Okihumky.
ASSIOLA,[24] (Powell) 5th do. and sub-chf.,	Ouithlocko.
COA HAJO,[25] (Alligator) 6th do. -	Negro town.
MOKE IS SHE LARNI, (One that sleeps,) 7th do. - - - - -	Wahoo Swamp.
CATSHA TUSTE-NUGGEE, (Little cloud) 8th do. - - - - -	Ouithlocko.

SUB-CHIEFS.

BILLY JOHN, - - - -	Pilaklakaha.
ALABARTU HAJO, (Creeping baby) -	Long Swamp.
TUSTINUC HAJO, (Half moon)- -	do.
ACOLA HAJO, - - - -	do.
WE FLOCCO MATTA, - -	Okihumky.
KOSKI UKA, (Fire stick) - - -	do.
ECHU MATTA, (Water serpent)	do.
TOPALARGEE, (The wonder) - -	do.
HATHOW MATTA, (Sea shell) - -	do.
CHAR CHAR TOSNUSK, (Fallen tree)	Ouithlocko.
COSA TUSTENUGGEE, (Yellow bull)	Wahoo Swamp.
CHETI HAIOLA, (Rising Star) - -	Ouithlocko.
POWSHAILA, (The dwarf) -	do.

SUB CHIEFS				RESIDENCE.
EMATHLOCHEE,	-	-	-	Minatti.
TA COSA FIXICO,	-	-	-	Chetucksta.
YAHA FIXICO, (Crazy eagle)		-		do.
TUSTINUC YAHA,	-	-	-	Hitchitipusy.
CONCHATTEE,	-	-	-	do.
TUSTENUGGEE,	-	-	-	Wahoo Swamp.

The chiefs have the command of parties numbering from fifty to two hundred warriors, which are subdivided, when the sub-chiefs, according to their influence or merits, are apportioned their command; so that we find, in some instances, one chief with a small number of warriors, whilst another has control of ten times as many. The same applies to the sub-chief, while, in some instances, he has no command of warriors.

The names of the friendly chiefs who were in favour of recognizing the validity of the treaty of 1832, and of conforming to its provisions, are as follows:

CHARLEY AMATHLA, (killed by Assiola and
    others) Chief of   -   -   -   Witamky.
YAHA AMATHLA, sub do.   -   -   do.
HOLATA AMATHLA, Chief of -   -   Sitarky.
COSATCHI AMATHLA, sub do.   -   do.
FUCTA LUSTA HAJO, (Black craggy clay)
    Principal War Chief at one time,   Chicuchatty.
OTULKEE OHALA, (Big warrior) Chief of   do.
CONHATKEE MICO   -   -   -   Hitchitipusy.

It will be seen that the standing of Assiola,[*] (Powell,) was, prior to the war, much inferior to a number of the other chiefs,

---

[*] *This* is the correct orthography of his name, which he has distinctly pronounced more than one hundred times in the presence of the gentleman before alluded to.

and although his *influence* was seemingly great, it was still less than that of Miconopy, Jumper, Holata Mico, Coa Hajo, Arpiucki, Abraham, and several others; but he was with the mass of warriors who were the anti-removal party, and themselves possessing as much influence as their chiefs; so that the marvellous [*sic*] reports of him, and the influence which it is supposed *he* exerts over the Indians is very exaggerated, and have their origin only in the bold, desperate and reckless *murders* which have been perpetrated by the band of Micosukees, of which he is a *sub-chief.* HOLATA MICO is the chief leader of that band, and decidedly superior to Assiola in every point of view. The latter is a *Red Stick* (*not* Micosukee) by descent, and prior to the breaking out of hostilities was leader of but seven warriors.[*] His talents are not above mediocre; and he was never known, by those who were most intimate with him, to possess any of the nobler qualities which adorn the Indian character: all his dealings have been characterized by a low, sordid, and contracted spirit, which often produced difficulties with those with whom he had intercourse. Perverse and obstinate in his disposition, he would frequently oppose measures which it was to the interest of his people that he should advocate. The principal chiefs were favourable to the project of emigration, but the *mass* of warriors were opposed; it was therefore "neck or nothing;" and as Holata Mico and his band (with Assiola) were the first to be removed by the provisions of the treaty, and these warriors having been averse to the project from the first, they sowed discord among the others by

---

[*] As I was informed by *Fucta Lusta Hajo,* a friendly chief.

11

threatening to murder all who should advocate the measure; and it was doubtless through *fear* that Assiola joined the hostile party after the pledge he had made to leave the country. This description of Assiola may perhaps serve to disabuse the public mind of the "noble character," "lofty bearing," "the high soul," "amazing powers" and "magnanimity" of the "Micosukee chief."

TRUE CAUSES OF THE WAR.

As early as 1821, General Jackson, then Governor of Florida, strongly urged government to adopt measures to send back all the Creek Indians who had, in 1814 and 1818, fled from their nation and taken up their abode in Florida, as he not only deemed it an encroachment upon the rights of the other tribes, but foresaw that an increase of Indian population in that country must sooner or later inevitably produce the most unpleasant consequences. In 1822, Col. Joseph M. White, the representative of that territory, addressed a letter to the Secretary of War, insisting with great earnestness upon the adoption of those suggestions as the only efficient mode to give peace and quiet to the country; but these recommendations were so far disregarded that a treaty was held with these Indians, together with others on the peninsula, on the 18th Sept. 1823, at Camp Moultrie,[*26] which stipulated for their continuance in the territory during twenty years. They were thereby established in the very heart of the country, and their claims to lands acknowledged, to which, in reality, they had not a shadow of title.

The synopsis of that treaty is as follows:

The Seminole Indians relinquished all their claim to lands in Florida, with the exception of a tract, estimated to contain

---

[*] See Map.

about five millions of acres, within the limits of which they bound themselves to continue.

The United States were to pay the Indians two thousand dollars to aid them in the removal of their families and stock from their respective towns to the new reservation; to furnish them with articles of husbandry, stock, &c., to the amount of six thousand dollars; to furnish them with corn, meat, and salt, for one year after they were collected within the limits assigned them; to pay them four thousand five hundred dollars for the improvements which they surrendered with their lands; to allow them one thousand dollars per annum for a blacksmith, and one thousand dollars per annum for a school fund; these two last allowances to be made for twenty successive years.

In less than a year after these obligations had been exchanged, complaints were already made to the authorities of depredations on the property of the whites—their fields having been plundered and their cattle driven off and killed—and, as may be readily imagined, these outrages were attributed to the Indians. How far they may have been actually culpable in having *first* commenced these depredations, I will not pretend to determine, but I am inclined to believe, from the mass of evidence furnished me, that the whites have not been backward in applying Indian property to their own uses, whenever it may have suited their convenience; and as the laws were alone favourable to the whites in consequence of the exclusion of Indian evidence in courts of justice, they thought they had a doubtless right to do with the Indian, or his property, as they might think proper. I will in this place cite some few instances, which show the justice of this inference, and which will also prove how little attention has been devoted to the interest of these unfortunate people, even after the most solemn pledge on the part of our government to protect them in their rights, and to regard their property as inviolate.

The agent for the Indians, in a letter to Governor Duval,[27] says—"Three white men have trespassed upon the Indian reserve, and committed violence upon the persons of several Indians; and I have in consequence left notices with the magistrate, to be served by the officer who served the warrants, directing the intruders to leave the Indian reserve in one day after the service of the notice." Now here is official proof of the justice which is practised towards these unfortunate beings. The intruders, who have been guilty of an aggravated assault upon the red people, are directed to leave the Indian reserve, in *one day after* the receipt of the notice. Why were they not taken into custody and subjected to punishment for violating the laws? why grant them one whole day, when it afforded them an opportunity of glutting their revenge upon the poor wretches who had had the misfortune already to endure a painful outrage at their hands? I say, why were they not legally punished, and ordered to leave immediately?

Two men by the name of Robinson and Wilburn, belonging to Georgia, availed themselves of the excitement produced by the late hostilities to circulate unfavourable reports of a chief called *Econchatta Mico*, a high minded and very honourable man, stating that he was about to join the hostile Indians; by this means they succeeded in dispossessing the chief and his people of their fire arms and other means of defence, when these scoundrels took forcible possession of twenty of his slaves, amounting in value to about fifteen thousand dollars and carried them off to New Orleans.

Another influential chief, *Emachitochustern,* commonly called John Walker, was robbed of a number of slaves in a somewhat similar manner. After making an appeal to the government agent, without the least chance of redress, he says—"I don't like to make any trouble or to have any quarrel with white people, but if they will trespass on my lands and rights, I must defend myself the best way I can, and if they do come again they must bear the consequences. But is there no *civil* law to protect me? are the negroes belonging to me to be stolen away publicly in the face of all law and justice—carried off and sold to fill the pockets of these land pirates? Douglass and his company have hired a man who has two large trained dogs for the purpose, to come here and take off others. He is from Mobile, and follows catching negroes."

Colonel John Blount,[28] another estimable chief, was inhumanly beaten by a party of white men, who robbed him of several hundred dollars; he made application to the authorities, but the villains were allowed to escape.

These facts show how mild and forbearing the Seminoles have acted under the most trying circumstances; and even when their property has been assailed in this way, they have, in numerous instances, refrained from making resistance; their hands were bound, as the severest punishment awaited any attack *they* might make upon the intruders, even though circumstances justified it; but as the Indian's evidence could not be received in a court of justice, the white man's oath would condemn him to the most torturing punishment.

I now subjoin a letter which was approved of by ten of the Seminole towns, and it cannot be doubted, that it is an honest relation of facts: it tells us in language pathetic and feeling, an artless tale, and it cannot be misunderstood.

To the Commanding Officer at Fort Hawkins.

DEAR SIR:

"Since the last war, after you sent us word that we must quit the war, our red people have come over on this side. The white people have carried all the red people's cattle off. Bernard's[29] son was here, and I asked him what to do about it—he told me to go to the head white man and complain. I did so, and there was no head white man, and there was no law in the case. *The whites first began to steal from us,* and there's nothing said about that, but great complaints about what the Indians do. It is now three years since white people killed three Indians; and since, they have killed three more; and since, one more. *The white people killed our red people first*—the Indians took satisfaction. There are three men that the red people have not taken satisfaction for yet. There is nothing said about what white people do—but all that the Indians do is brought up. The cattle that we are accused of taking, were cattle that the *white people took from us*—our young men went out and brought them back with the *same marks and brands.*"

In proof of the substance of this letter, I have been told that the hoard of desperadoes who infest the borders of the Indian reserve and hang around its skirts, frequently prompt the wretched drunken and worthless Indian to drive the cattle of their neighbours within, or outside of the line, as the case may be, to a considerable distance from the owner's lands, where the white man would meet him, and with a quart or two of rum pay him for his trouble; and then, by driving their ill gotten gain to another section of country, would barter them off without a probability of detection. This has been mentioned to me by several respectable citizens of Florida, who have, more or less, suffered in this way. It is also said that the new settlers would admit the Indians to lounge familiarly in their kitchens—on their beds—eat at their tables—and that this continued as long as the settler had any use for the Indian; but the moment he could serve them no longer he was driven off, treated with the greatest cruelty, and has often been found, by others of their tribe, lying severely wounded and helpless in the woods. Let no one say this picture is too highly coloured, for undoubted evidence of these facts can be had by any one who will take the trouble to inquire.

A Mr. Walker, of Alachua county says, in a letter to the Indian agent—"There were several of my neighbours out in the woods the other day, and were fired on by the Indians, and three of them badly wounded, for which they demand satisfaction of you, you being the proper person; and if they get no other satisfaction they are determined to take it on themselves," &c.

General Thompson replies—"I have made a demand on the nation for the Indians who committed the outrage. Tomorrow the chiefs are to assemble for the purpose of ordering the delivery of the perpetrators over to the civil authorities. I am much pleased to learn that you with your command, and a company from an adjoining county, intend to scour the country on the Indian boundary in the direction you indicated, as I have no doubt it will have a salutary effect upon the Mickasukee Indians, who are the most troublesome of any belonging to the nation. You are aware of the delicate character of our relations with these people, and that all causeless irritation should be avoided. Should you fall in with any, *try* to get possession of them without bloodshed."

From the character of Mr. Walker's communication, it would seem as though his neighbours had been fired on by the Indians without having given them the least provocation, and that the innocent neighbours had not even made resistance after the attack was commenced, although one Indian was *killed*, and another very dangerously wounded. Let us take a view of the examination of the Indians who escaped unhurt, and then we shall discover who the really guilty were, and whether the accused were not alone acting on the defensive. It will be remembered, that this examination takes place, not in a court room and in presence of their accusers, but at a time and place, (although it did not render the obligation of speaking the truth less sacred,) when, had they been disposed to avoid the penalty for crossing beyond their boundary, they could have done so; for as they were not opposed by other testimony, they might have given such a colouring to their story as would most effectually have tended to their vindication: but they evidently tell the straight forward, honest truth.

Examination of Wacooche Hajo, Sapokitee, We-ha-sit-kee

and Capicha Hajo, some of the Indians who formed the party that was engaged in the rencontre [*sic*] in Alachua county, on the 19th day of June, 1835.

THEIR STATEMENT.

Wacooche Hajo, Sapokite, Wehalitkee, Fuxe, and Saw-tichee, of Long Swamp, went beyond the Indian boundary near Kanapaha pond, in Alachua county. Before they marched there they killed a cow (which did not belong to them,) in the neighbourhood of Deamond's pond. When they got within three miles of Kenapaha [*sic*], near a sink hole, where there is water, they encamped. Another party of Indians, viz., Capicha Hajo, Chokikee and Hithlomee, from Big Swamp, who had been upon the Santafee [Santa Fe] river, met them there and encamped a short distance from the first party; that two of the Long Swamp Indians, to wit, Lecotichee and Fuxe, went out hunting in the morning; the other six, to wit, Wacoochee Hajo, Sapokitee, Wehalitkee, Capicha Hajo, Chokikee, and Hith-lomee, were together about 12 o'clock at one of the camps, when a party of whites arrived at the camp where the six Indians were together, *took their guns from three of them, examined their packs, and commenced whipping them,* and the Indians ran off. One of them ran but a short distance, when he was called by the whites. The whites commenced whipping him again; he called to another Indian who had also ran off; at that crisis the two Indians who had been out hunting, to wit, Lecotichee and Fuxe were approaching the camp, and commenced firing at the party of whites. The whites returned the fire, *killed* Fuxe and wounded Lechotichee severely, the other

20

three from Long Swamp were disarmed before the firing commenced. The three from Big Swamp, who were at the camp of the Long Swamp Indians when the whites arrived, and had left their guns at their own camp, ran off when the firing commenced, without their guns. After the whites had left the scene of action, one or two of the Indians went back and got their guns. Three guns were taken by the whites before the firing commenced, and were carried off by them. But two Indians, to wit, Fuxe and Lechotiche fired, and they fired two or three times each.

June 25, 1835—*Afternoon.*

EXAMINATION OF CHOKIKEE AND HITHLOMEE.

They were with Capicha Hajo, and had been upon the Santafee river. They met Wacooche Hajo, and four other Indians at a sink hole where there is water, about three miles from Kanapaha pond. Two of the Long Swamp Indians were out hunting; the three Big Swamp Indians were at the camp of the other party, making six at that camp. About 12 o'clock a party of white men came upon that camp; the whites began to whip the Indians, and about the time they commenced whipping the second one, the two who were out hunting, to wit, Lechotichee and Fuxe or Fixoneechee, approached the camp and commenced firing on the whites; and when they were in the act of firing the second round, they, (the said Chokikee and Hithlomee ran off and did not stop until they reached their town,) Wacoochee Hajo, Sapokitee, Weehalitkee, Capicha Hajo and the said Chokikee and Hithlomee, were alone together at the same camp when the party of whites, consisting

of seven, came upon them. Capiche Hajo and the said Chokikee and Hithlomee had left their guns at their own camp. The
other three, to wit, Wacoochee Hajo, Sapokitee and Wehalitkee were disarmed by the whites, before the other two, to
wit, Lechotichee and Fixe or Fixonechee, appeared and commenced firing, and the whites had the guns of said Indians
stacked against a tree, where they were guarded by some of
the whites. There were but eight Indians in the whole, and
none fired but the two before stated; the others were disarmed,
and could not have fired had they been so disposed."

These six Indians were kept confined thirty-three days for
the purpose of giving the complainants every opportunity to
satisfy their revenge, but the proof was so unfavourable to a
successful prosecution that they deemed it wisest to "dodge
the question" and be content that they escaped so well. The
instant a demand was made for the aggressors, the chiefs were
prompt to arrest and transfer them to the authorities to be dealt
with accordingly. I will now refer my readers to the letter of
General Thompson, in reply to Mr. Walker's. It cannot be denied, that the delegation of such authority—as the General's
letter certainly sanctions—to a body of men, whose feelings
were already excited by a previous rencontre [sic] with the
Indians, must be attended with the worst consequences. It
was, to say the least of it, rash and imprudent; for General
Thompson was well aware of the intense feeling existing
throughout the nation, growing out of the late aggressions, and
the near approach of the period of emigration, and that "all
causeless irritation should be avoided;" yet, in the very face of
these his own sentiments, he grants permission to the friends
of the disappointed men to carry out their spirit of retaliation

and revenge. But if it were necessary to have a guard to patrol the Indian boundary in order to keep the Indians within the reserve, why not commission the United States' troops for the purpose, who could have no cause to act illiberally towards them? Why should the command of Capt. Walker, or of any other man, in time of peace, be allowed to traverse the country to chastise the poor strolling red man, who, thoughtlessly, may have ventured beyond the boundary line in quest of game, or perhaps have been searching for his own goods? Why did not these disinterested creatures go to the peninsula, where they could have detected hundreds of the "hungry freebooters?" but perhaps the real object of their search, or "scout," could not there be found. For my own part, I can scarce ascribe the purest motives to these volunteer *protectors* of other men's property, whose paramount duty it was to remain at home and take care of their own; and I am therefore strongly inclined to believe that they anticipated the discovery of *other* stragglers, with certain *marks* and *brands, not* belonging to the outside of the boundary line, which, if intercepted in their perambulations, would perhaps be some compensation for their trouble and loss of time in so dutifully serving—the public!

A party of gentlemen who volunteered in the cause against the Indians, but in consequence of their honorable wounds had been discharged, were on their way from Fort Drane to Black Creek. Having been long strangers to fresh meat, one of the party was induced to pick a calf from a herd that was running through the woods. A few moments after, an individual by the name of Daniels, whose name is attached to a petition to the

President, praying for an early removal of the Indians, came up and demanded pay for it, alleging that it was his property. One of the gentlemen asked him the price of it. He replied, "three dollars; but," said he, "if you will report, or return it, to the quarter master at Black Creek, so that I can get remunerated for it by the government, it will all be right." To this, assent was given. But thinking 'a bird in hand, is worth two in the bush,' he recollected that he had returned his cattle to the government agent before hostilities commenced, and he therefore thought it would be better if the gentleman paid him now. One of the drivers said the charge was exorbitant—he could buy all the calves of that size in Alachua, at one dollar a head. My hero then fell to one dollar and fifty cents, which was readily paid, (and so would three dollars, had they been certain he was the right owner.) As the party were about to move, the honest Mr. Daniels remarked, "Well, gentlemen, you've paid me the *full value* of that calf, but you see as I've lost a good many things which the government won't pay me for, I must make it up on my cattle."

I have related the story at length, merely to illustrate the character of some men in that county, and which conclusively shows that, if they would thus attempt to defraud the government, who have means of detection and the power to inflict punishment therefor [sic], with what certainty such men as Daniels could carry on a system of corruption and fraud where the power of investigation is stifled.

Col. Gad Humphreys,[30] formerly an Indian agent, was elected a member of the Legislative Council of Florida, in consequence of his urging that the territorial jurisdiction should be extended over the Indians, in which case instead of submitting negro claims to the United States, the only proper source to appeal to, the prosecutions could be made in the territorial courts with a confident expectation of success, as Indian evidence would not be received except in opposing Indian claims. Col. Humphreys is himself a claimant for negroes, under a bill of sale from a desperate and notorious scoundrel by name of Dexter.[31] When Humphreys was Indian agent, the owner of these negroes, who is a woman by the name of Culekeechowa, applied to him for the recovery of them from Dexter, who was then about to dispose of them, which Humphreys promised to do; but instead of claiming them for the owner he made a purchase of the slaves for himself, alleging that he did so to prevent their being carried off to Charleston. Part of the negroes, after they grew up and learned the state of the case, went back to their Indian owner, when Humphreys solicited General Thompson to procure their return to him; but the facts of the case so strongly indicated the right of Culekeechowa to the negroes, as she had never received a compensation for them, that Thompson dismissed the application of Humphreys and referred the subject to the decision of government. Col. Humphreys is also a claimant in another case under similar circumstances, but in conjunction with others that were submitted to the Legislative Council, was set aside by that body.

A man by the name of Floyd was employed by an Indian woman to recover some negroes for her, and instead of presenting a mere power of attorney for her signature, she found, alas! it was a *bill of sale* for all of her negroes! Another individual was requested by Miconopy, Governor of the Seminoles, to draw a piece of writing for him, to which, without suspicion of its character, he attached his name; it was soon after discovered to be a conveyance of a large tract of land!

These are but a few of the very many cases of this description with which the poor Indians have had to contend, and they are still held in reserve in the hope that they may yet obtain a majority of two thirds to extend the jurisdiction of the territory in defiance of executive authority. Should they succeed in so doing, these claims will be substantiated, and the descendants of negroes who have passed hereditarily from generation to generation, will be alike subjected to the fraudulent control of these men; hence the object of this combination to interpose every obstacle to removal, and by thwarting the plans of the government they will keep the Indians where they are, until their possessions may be wrested from them under the authority which they are aiming to establish.

Another source of vexation and great irritation is from the numerous and vile impositions of a pecuniary nature which have been practised upon these poor wretches.—One of the government agents was a delinquent to them for a considerable amount. He robbed the principal interpreter of the nation, a very influential black chief by the name of *Abraham*, of several hundred dollars, by getting a receipt from him without paying the money, under the plea that it was necessary to send the receipt to Washington, where it was filed to the credit of the agent. Several other Indians of influence were robbed in a similar manner; and when they demanded the money from the succeeding agent, they were told that the government would not pay them. Is not this an unsound principle to adopt in our intercourse with the Indians? Is it just or honourable for us to send *our own* agents among them, without their approval, and not hold ourselves responsible for their conduct? If we were indebted to a nation, and the funds are sent through an agent to pay over, and he neglects to do so, are we not still liable, and would not a civilized power still hold us responsible? Then if, as Mr. Secretary Cass says, "that the treaty making powers (of course all others) with the Indian tribes have been placed upon the same footing and to the same extent that it is with the civilized powers," are not these poor Indians entitled to the benefit of it? Then why withhold from them their just dues, and excite in them revengeful feelings?

But, separate and apart from the general principle which should govern in all cases, the one in reference to Abraham, from mere matter of policy and expediency, and for the sake of securing his friendship and influence, which was unbounded and was known by the Department to be so, should not have been permitted to pass by unnoticed. His fondness for money amounted almost to avarice; he had rendered important services to the government in the capacity of an Interpreter, and for which this money was due him; and to refuse him remuneration, it could not but be foreseen would prove detrimental to the best interests of the Indians, and mar the prospect of emigration.

The annoyance arising from the Indians being so near the settlements of the whites, and their alleged depredations, resulted in petition after petition to the President praying for their removal, at an earlier period than that prescribed in the treaty of Camp Moultrie. These memorials, signed by many respectable citizens of Alachua county, were so far regarded by the President that a new treaty was immediately decided upon. For this purpose Col. Gadsden,[32] a highly respectable and intelligent citizen of Florida, was appointed a commissioner to make known to the Indians the views of the government, and, if possible, to secure a new arrangement.

Colonel Gadsden went into the nation, and, on the 8th of April, 1832, had an interview with Miconopy and a few other chiefs, upon the subject of a removal of their tribe west of the Mississippi. As might have been anticipated, he found little objection to the proposal, as from the almost starved condition of a large number of the Indians, in consequence of a failure in the crop of the preceding year, and having been subsisting for the previous three months upon the palmetto cabbage, roots, &c., it may be readily conceived they would have embraced *any* proposition or measure that would be the means of contributing to the amelioration of their wants. The chief Miconopy said, he wished all his people to hear what their father in Washington had to communicate to them, but their warriors were out on their annual hunt, and many of them in the lower part of the peninsula—one hundred and fifty to two hundred miles from their home—so that it would be difficult to collect them immediately; he therefore wished Col. Gadsden to defer the communication for thirty days. This request was complied with, and in the mean time orders were issued for the distribution of corn to assist them in planting, as the season had far advanced, and to afford some few provisions to enable the warriors to return from the woods to their towns.

The principal body of Indians having assembled, according to appointment, at Payne's Landing, on the Ocklawaha river, (*see map*) Col. Gadsden met them on the 8th of May, 1832, in order to negotiate on the subject of his mission. Having opened the views of the government in relation to the disposition of their tribe, Col. Gadsden discovered that there would be great difficulty in accomplishing the negotiation in accordance with his instructions. He however succeeded in obtaining their consent to the conditions proposed, except in some immaterial particulars, provided a deputation of seven confidential chiefs, whom they should select, reported favourably to them of the country. The leading features of this treaty were:[33]

1st. The Seminole Indians to relinquish their claim to the tract of land reserved for them by the second article of the Camp Moultrie treaty, containing four million thirty-two thousand six hundred and forty acres, and to remove west of the Mississippi, and there become a constituent portion of the Creek tribe.

2d. The United States to pay the Seminole Indians fifteen thousand four hundred dollars, as a consideration for the improvements which they abandoned with their lands; and a further sum to the two blacks, Abraham and Cudjoe,[34] of two hundred dollars each.

3d. Each of the Indians to be furnished with a blanket and a homespun frock, and a sufficient quantity of corn, meat and salt, for their support for one year after their arrival in the new country.

4th. The blacksmith, provided for in the Camp Moultrie treaty, to be continued ten years longer, at one thousand dollars per year.

5th. The United States to pay them an additional annuity of three thousand dollars for fifteen successive years after their arrival in the west; which sum, together with the four thousand dollars stipulated for in the Camp Moultrie Treaty, (making seven thousand dollars per annum) to be paid to the Creek nation with their annuities.

6th. In order to relieve the Seminoles from the vexatious demands on them for slaves and other property, the United States stipulated to have the same investigated, and to liquidate such as were satisfactorily established, provided the amount did not exceed seven thousand dollars.

This treaty was executed on the 9th of May 1832, and signed by the following chiefs, viz:—

Holata Amathla.
Jumper.
Fucta Lusta Hajo, (Black craggy clay, generally called, Black dirt.)
Charley Amathla.
Coa Hajo, (Alligator.)
Arpiucki, (Sam Jones.)
Yaha Hajo, (Mad wolf.)
Miconopy, head Chief and Governor of the Seminoles.
Tokosa Amathla, (John Hicks.)
Catsha Tustenuggee, (Little cloud.)
Holata Mico, (Blue king.)
Hitchiti Mico, (Broken sticks.)
Enehah, (The buzzard.)
Yaha Amathla Chupko.
Moke Is She Larni, (One that sleeps.)

The first seven chiefs were deputed to visit and explore the new country, selected for their future residence. Abraham, their firm and faithful adherent and interpreter, accompanied them. Major Phagan,[35] formerly Indian agent in Florida, was authorised to accompany the delegation, and commissioners were appointed to meet and attend on them during the examination of the country.

The delegation having approved of the country, the ratification of the treaty, on their part, was confirmed by the seven chiefs in presence of the commissioners, at Fort Gibson,[36] La., [Arkansas] on the 28th March, 1833, which was to be considered binding on the Seminole nation. The chiefs however were only authorized to proceed to an examination of the lands, and report the results of their mission to a general council of the nation, which was to be convened on their return; and they, therefore, exceeded the instructions and the authority granted them, by affixing their consent to the obligations of the treaty, without first consulting their people.

The commissioner, Col. Gadsden, in a letter to the Secretary of War, says—"There is a condition prefixed to the agreement, without assenting to which the Florida Indians *most positively refused* to negotiate for their removal west of the Mississippi. Even with the condition annexed, there was a reluctance (which with some difficulty was overcome) on the part of the Indians, to bind themselves by *any* stipulations before a knowledge of facts and circumstances would enable them to judge of the advantages or disadvantages of the disposition the government of the United States wished to make of them. They were finally *induced* however to assent to the agreement." Again, he says—"The payment for property alleged to have been plundered was the subject more pressed by the Indians, and in yielding to their wishes on this head, a limitation has been fixed in a sum, which I think, however, will probably cover all demands which can be satisfactorily proved. Many of the claims are for negroes, said to have been enticed away from their owners during the protracted Indian disturbances, of which Florida has been for years the theatre. The Indians allege that the depredations were mutual, that they have suffered in the same degree, and that most of the property claimed, was taken as reprisal for property of equal value lost by them. They could not, therefore, yield to the justice of restitution solely on their part, and probably there was no better mode of terminating the difficulty than by that provided for in the treaty now concluded. The final ratification of the treaty will depend upon the opinion of the seven chiefs selected to explore the country west of the Mississippi river. *If* that corresponds to the description given, or is equal to the expectations formed of it, there will be no difficulty on the part of the Seminoles. If the Creeks however raise any objections, this will be a sufficient protext [*sic*] on the part of some of the Seminole deputation to oppose the execution of the whole arrangement for removal."

Here we have the most cogent proof that the commissioner himself, by his own acknowledgment, knew that the delegation of chiefs had no authority to ratify the treaty on the part of the Seminole nation, but that they were to make a report to the nation on their return; and if the report corresponded to the description given, or was equal to the expectations formed by *the Seminoles,* then there would be no difficulty in consummating the treaty; and it is evident that a suspicion was lurking in the mind of Col. Gadsden, even at the very moment the treaty was executed, that insuperable objections existed on the part of the Indians to a removal, and that it was indeed very doubtful whether, under *any* circumstances, they would voluntarily leave Florida, or that their removal could be effected without resort to military force. He had even *exceeded* the instructions of government, and still found that it was alone by exaggerated promises and representations, which he thought might in part be realized, that the Indians were, even then, "*induced*" to concur in the agreement. At all events, they have expressed a misconception, on their part, of the true terms of the treaty, and were not, therefore, bound by its stipulations. The language used by Col. Gadsden certainly evinces much labour on his part towards the accomplishment of his mission. That he was determined, *per fas aut nefas,* [by lawful or unlawful means] to render a satisfactory account to those, at least, by whom he was commissioned, is apparent throughout all his correspondence on the subject; indeed, he has been a most faithful agent in the matter, as far as our own government views were concerned, and is a most excellent man; in every point of view he commands my warmest respect, and I should reprove myself if I thought he was done injustice to by these remarks. He was requested by the *government* to drive as good a bargain as he could, but not to exceed the limits prescribed in the letter of instructions, and therefore, if illiberality was displayed in the provisions, the blame rests with the author, and not the agent.

The importance of an early ratification of this treaty was earnestly pressed upon the attention of our government by Col. Gadsden and others, under the apprehension that, if delay occurred in procuring the necessary appropriations for the removal of the one-third of the Indians, which was stipulated should take place within the following year, (1833,) serious obstacles might be thrown in the way to embarrass the operations and thwart the policy of the government, by a class of evil disposed persons whose interest would be injuriously affected by the Indians leaving that country. Two years, however, were suffered to elapse before its validity was acknowledged; and some time after that, before appropriations were made. In the meantime dissatisfaction was engendered, (if it did not exist before,) and the treaty was openly and publicly denounced as "a white man's treaty," and they said that they did not intend it should be binding on them.

Part of the small military force which had been stationed there, was, at an inauspicious moment, withdrawn from the territory; a change of agents had taken place; the local agent had been absent from the nation for nearly a year: Major Phagan had robbed and deceived them; which, taken in connexion [sic] with the inaction on the part of our government towards a fulfillment of the stipulations of the treaty, induced them to regard it as an indifference, on our part, to carry it into effect.

How far this conclusion may have been justifiable by existing circumstances I am unprepared to say; although it would seem that the right or justice of coercing them to a removal after a failure on our part to acknowledge the treaty within a reasonable time, has been questioned, and already a subject of inquiry and consideration at the government quarters. I cannot perhaps better serve my readers than by inserting a letter from

34

the Hon. John H. Eaton[37] to the Secretary of War, on this subject, and which will probably indicate the light in which the Indians have viewed it.

Tallahassee, March 8, 1835.

"DEAR SIR:—I have received your letter, with its enclosures, relative to the removing the Seminole Indians, under the provisions of the treaty of 1832, but which was not ratified until 1834. I pray you, does not this circumstance raise a doubt whether, by strict rule, the treaty can be considered to be valid and binding?—Our Indian compacts must be construed and be controlled by the rules which civilized people practice, because in all our actions with them, we have put the treaty making machinery in operation precisely in the same way, and to the same extent, that it is employed with the civilized powers of Europe. The rule practised [*sic*] upon us, has been, and is, that the ratification shall take place within either an agreed time, or a reasonable time. When Florida was ceded in 1819, the *Cortes* failed to interchange ratifications within the prescribed time, and afterwards, at a subsequent session, it was assented to by the Spanish Cortes. The sense of this government was, that the first ratification made by the Senate was inoperative;—and again the subject was submitted by Mr. Monroe,[38] for the action and approval of the Senate. This appears to me to be a precedent which runs parallel with this Indian compact. It says, one-third shall remove the first year, viz., early as practicable in 1833; and one-third in the next, and the next 1834-35. Now, until 1834, when the ratification took place, the treaty was a dead letter. It is in their power now to plead and say, we were ready in 1833 and 1834, and hearing nothing of your determination, we had a right to suppose that you did not mean to stand by the treaty, and accordingly our minds have changed. With civilized nations, I think the plea would be available; and if so, the Indian should have the benefit of it.

"Were these people willing, voluntarily, to remove, (though such seems not to be the case,) the whole difficulty would be cured, and no evil could arise. But as military force is about to be resorted to, it is material that the government, before making such appeal, be satisfied that right and justice is on their side, and that they are not engaged in the execution of a treaty, which, if void, is no part of the law of the land.

"The people here want the lands on which they reside, and they will urge a removal *fas aut nefas*; and the Big Swamp which, in the treaty, is declared to be the first of their country to be vacated, is of high repute, and is that on which the eyes of speculators are fixed.—But whether they shall have it this year or the next, or the next thereafter, is of less importance to the country than that anything should be done calculated to impair the character of the government for justice, and for equitable and fair dealing. Whence the necessity of any speedy removal? Presently, if let alone, these Indians will go of their own accord, because, they cannot avoid it. To say is to starve: and nature and its demands will soon tell them more and better, and more convincing things on this subject than you and the President can write.

"The employing a military force will be an act of war, and the Indians will imbody [*sic*] and fight in their defence. In this event, you will want such an imposing force as shall overawe resistance. The few companies you have ordered, will not produce this result. They will serve but to begin the fight, and to awaken angry feelings, so that in the sequel, the militia will have to be called, which will end in the butchery of these miserable people. Send a strong, imposing, *regular force,* which can be commanded, and prevented from doing more than actually is needed to be done: and then that force, judiciously acting and forbearing, may do much. But send only a handful of men, and difficulties will come upon you.

"The preferred and preferable course I think, will be to send amongst them active and intelligent men, to *court* them to what is right, in the hope that, during the year, their minds may be so prepared as to be induced to depart during November at least, that they may reach their homes in time to raise corn the succeeding year.—On the whole, and to conclude a tiresome letter, I offer this advice: Avoid the exercise of *force* as long as possible, and let it be the only, the last sad alternative, and then let not, by any means, the *militia* be appealed to; they will breed mischief!

"With great respect,

"J. H. EATON.

"HON. L. CASS, *Secretary of War.*"

In reply to the sensible suggestions of Governor Eaton, Mr. Secretary Cass, says—"The question presented in your letter respecting the validity of the obligation of the Seminole Indians to remove from Florida, has been submitted to the Attorney General, and that officer has decided that the obligation of the treaty is not affected by the delay which has taken place, but that the Indians may be required to remove in the years 1835, '36, and 37."

For my own part, I would not dare argue the right or wrong of this decision of Mr. Attorney Butler,[39] respecting the removal in those particular years, but as that point has been esteemed sufficiently important for the grave consideration of wiser heads, I wonder that the authority for the removal *of the entire tribe of Seminole Indians, simultaneously*, in the year 1836, has not been questioned. By what principle of law is that order governed? Or is it the decree of "THE GOVERN-MENT," that the laws of the United States must be so interpreted as to suit our peculiar circumstances?—I pause for reply.

I cannot but regard the treaty at Payne's Landing* as having been the main cause of all those excesses which have led to the present war; and, if so, it only adds another melancholy proof to the many on record, that hard and unconscionable terms, extorted from them while in distress, under promises never to be realized, has only served to whet and stimulate revenge and to give to old hostilities, not yet extinguished, greater exasperation and ferocity. A treaty thus obtained from an unfortunate and wretched people, without means, and reduced to the last extremity of distress, whose miserable existence we had to preserve by a voluntary distribution of food, could not—ought not to be relied on. The instant there was the slightest prospect of relief, from such unjust terms and severe *restrictions*, the oppressed party flew to arms, and they

---

* See page 29.

will spend the last drop of their blood rather than live in such degraded bondage.—Even if we again reduce them to submission, the expenses incurred in doing it, to say nothing of the human life sacrificed in the cause, will be one hundred times greater than it would have cost us had we granted them the conditions which they earnestly implored in the first instance.

A common ground of accusation against the faith and honesty of the Indian, is his total disregard of treaties and obligations, and the treacherous and instantaneous manner with which he will fly to the commencement of hostilities from a supposed injury. But the communication of the white man is too apt to be cold, distrustful and insulting; he does not treat the Indian with that confidence which is indispensable to real friendship. The finer feelings of his nature—his pride—his superstitions are disregarded; he thus feels himself deeply insulted,—which oftener prompts him to acts of hostility than the mere consideration of interest.

It has been his misfortune, from the earliest period of civilization, to contend, not only with the mercenary and very often wanton, warfare of the white people, by whom he has been despoiled of his lands, but the nobler qualities of his character have been overlooked. The settler has spurned him from his door—cast him "like a loath-some thing away," and treated him like a beast; not that he was guilty or had "sinned against man," but, then, the poor wanderer of the forest, the once undisputed lord of this soil, was ignorant. The rights of the Indian have not been properly appreciated;—they have been trampled under foot, and his feelings have been as little respected; consequently the cruelty of the Indian towards his prisoner has been increased since the colonist came.

"We were a happy people then,
Rejoicing in our hunter mood;
No footsteps of the pale faced men,
Had marred our forest solitude."

What was considered by them a mere compliance with the views of policy and superstition, is now regarded and turned into the gratification of vengeance. They are sensible of their approaching annihilation; they find the white man has usurped their domain, and made them an abject and degraded people— while the gradual destruction of their kindred but too plainly tells them that they are the last remnant of a once powerful tribe. In war the Indian has been regarded as a ferocious beast, and therefore life or death was a matter of mere precaution. He goes into battle smarting under manifold injuries and indignities which have been heaped upon him; and he is driven into madness and despair by the overwhelming ruin which results from a warfare with us.

"They waste us; aye, like an April snow
In the warm noon we shrink away."

We have set them the example of violence by burning their homes and laying waste their very slender means of subsistence, and yet it is a matter of surprise and wonder to us that the Indian is not more forbearing, moderate and magnanimous to those whose very acts have deprived him of his all, and left him to repine in wretchedness and misery!

We are prone to denounce the Indian as cowardly and treacherous because his mode of warfare differs from ours and is based on stratagem; but they are borne out in this and fully justified in it by their rude and uncultivated code of laws, which, from infancy, they are taught to cherish and respect. The noblest and bravest warrior esteems it no disgrace to lurk in silence and take every advantage of his foe; *his* greatest triumph is in the superior craft and sagacity which he displays in decoying, surprising and destroying his enemies; for the first and most *natural* principle in war is, to inflict the greatest injury on our enemy without giving him the chance to injure us, and this can be effected by stratagem only, whether it be exercised by civilized man, or by the rude and uneducated red man of the wilderness,—the *principle,* is the same.

One of the principal causes of hostility to emigration, and which early exhibited itself, was to be found in the large negro property held by the Seminole nation. Many of these negroes are claimed by the Creek Indians, under the treaty made with the latter in 1821, by which the United States agreed to pay to the citizens of Georgia such claims as might be established against the Creeks for depredations committed, and slaves detained by them; and it is alleged by the Creeks that a large number of their negroes are in possession of the Seminoles and are unjustly withheld from them. The latter, however, contend, that they are their hereditary possessions, to which the Creeks have no title, and if they hold any claims against the Seminole nation, they must come under the provisions in the sixth article of the treaty of Payne's Landing, which stipulates for the payment of those claims by the United States.

The frequent and pressing demands of the Creeks have inspired a distrust with the Seminoles, that so soon as they became amalgamated with the former, this species of property would be forcibly wrested from them by the operations of the Creek National Council; as their minority in that body, and perhaps, total seclusion therefrom, would render remonstrances fruitless and resistance out of the question.

Under this view of the case, and in order to guard against these encroachments on their rights, the Seminoles solicited the government to apportion them a *separate* and *distinct tract* of land, where they might retain their sovereignty, free from the intervention and control of the tribe with which it was proposed to unite them; and that, by the appointment of a separate agent to protect them in their rights, it would be the means of preventing any just cause of complaint or dissatisfaction thereafter.

The treaty made with the Seminoles stipulated for a particular portion of the Creek country to be set apart for their occupancy; while the treaty formed with the Creeks authorized the location of the Seminoles among them, but provided for *no separate* allotment of their lands. In consequence of this the delegation of Creek chiefs, composed of Chilly M'Intosh, Roly M'Intosh, Foshutchee Mico and K. Lewis, addressed a letter to the Secretary of War, in which they remonstrated against the parcelling [*sic*] out of their lands, and expressed a desire that a new negotiation might be opened with the Seminoles, to induce them to settle *promiscuously*, among the Creeks, and become reunited under the same government and laws.—They also send word to the Seminoles, that while they were willing to receive them within their limits as a portion of their nation, they would not suffer them to enjoy a separate allotment of their soil.

It is very apparent, that the object of this movement of the Creeks was evidently with a view to dispossess the Seminoles, in the easiest manner, of their large negro property, to which the former had unsuccessfully urged a claim. This unwelcome news justly alarmed the Seminoles, and no doubt created that determined and invulnerable opposition to emigration which was so generally and strongly manifested throughout the nation.

On this subject the Indian agent, in a letter to the Department, advances the following opinion of General Clinch; "Having been long acquainted with these Indians, the character of the population surrounding them, and the localities of the country, so favourable to the corrupt views and projects of the rapaciously avaricious, he not only considers it very important that the Indians should be removed as early as practicable, but to *protect them against the possible avarice and ambition of their more numerous brethren of the west, they ought to be located at their new home in a separate body.* Candor requires me to say, that at least the protection which would be afforded to these people, *by settlement in a separate body, against the claim of the Creeks, for a large negro property now in this nation, is due to these people,* until an adjustment of the contested claim can be effected, and other personal rights and honorary distinctions secured to them.

Should an attempt be made by any of the conflicting claimants alluded to, or by any other person, with or without the aid of an act of the Legislative Council, extending the jurisdiction of the territory over these Indians, to wrest from Indian owners negroes so claimed, either before or after the Indians may commence their removal, by the intervention of the territorial authority, or the authority of any state through which they may pass, I shall feel it my duty to resist and perforce, if need be, any and all such attempts, which I am resolved to do, unless restrained by positive instructions from you. According to the intercourse laws, and the regulations of the Department of War, predicated upon those laws, all claims against these Indians should be submitted to the agent, and by him be reported to you. The withholding the claims alluded to, justifies the suspicion that the claimants design to evade the intercourse laws, and the regulations of your Department, by seizing upon some opportunity to avail themselves of territorial or state jurisdiction, and thus accomplish the contemplated fraud, by excluding Indian laws, and Indian evidence." And General Eaton, upon the same point observes, that the "Creeks west should be gotten to say, that the allotment made shall be for the exclusive, *separate* use of the Florida Indians; or the latter should be *prevailed* upon, *for some adequate compensation, to agree* to go and amalgamate with the Creeks.

The Secretary of War in replying to the humane and honourable suggestions of General Eaton, says—"The statement which you understand them to make respecting the occupation of a separate district in the Creek country west, *I consider of no sort of consequence.*"

To counteract these, (in the opinion of the goverment,) imaginary evils, it was then suggested to them that, by a sale of these negroes before they left Florida, they would augment their resources and could go into their new country without the dread of exciting the cupidity of the Creeks. But these Indians have always evinced great reluctance to parting with slaves: indeed the Indian loves his negro as much as one of his own children, and the sternest necessity alone would drive him to the parting: this recommendation was, therefore, viewed with evident alarm, and as the right of retaining possession of them was guaranteed by the commissioner, strong doubts were raised as to the sincerity of the pledge.

The Seminole Indians are poor agriculturists and husbandmen, and withal too indolent to till the ground, and, without their negroes, would literally starve: besides, should they dispose of them they could not be replenished in their new country. Again: the opposition of the slaves themselves to being sold to the whites would excite all their energies to prevent emigration, for they dread the idea of being transferred to sugar and cotton plantations where they must be subject to the surveillance of the overseer. His life among the Indians is one, compared with that of negroes under overseers, of luxury and ease; the demands upon him are very trifling, scarcely ever exceeding eight or ten bushels, from the crop, the remainder being applied to his own profit: they live separate, and often remote, from their owners, and enjoy an equal share of liberty. The negro is also much more provident and ambitious than his master, and the peculiar localities of the country eminently facilitate him in furnishing the Indian with rum and tobacco, which gives him a controlling influence over the latter, and, at the same time, affords him an immense profit; so that it can be easily imagined that the negroes would in no manner be benefited by the change. The intercourse laws prohibit the purchase of an Indian pony by a member of civilized society; and why?—Because the Indian is considered in a state of pupilage, and incapable of protecting himself against the arts and wiles of civilized man. If an Indian's interest in a pony is of so much importance, in the estimation of the government, as to require such strict guards to be thrown around it, the protection of his interest in his slave should be esteemed still more important, inasmuch as the latter is more valuable and useful to him than the former species of property. If, in the regulation of the sale of ponies, the United States exercise a rightful power, the obligation on them to guard the interest of the Indian in his slave is greatly more imposing.

But in total disregard of this accepted principle of protection to the Indians, framed under his own eye, "the government," is graciously pleased to confer upon "my friends" the sole and exclusive privilege of purchasing these negroes, and thereby opening the door to the most debased and corrupt species of speculations.—The permit to which I allude is to be found in the following endorsement of President Jackson on General Call's letter. I subjoin both:—

"Washington, March 22, 1835.

"SIR: I have received letters from some of my friends at Tallahassee to-day, requesting me, if possible, to obtain permission from the government to purchase the Indian right to certain negroes residing among the Seminoles, and *supposed*[*] to belong to the Indians. If there is no objection to such a purchase, and I presume there can be none, there is no measure which would contribute so much as this to the removal of the Indians. The negroes have great influence among the Indians; they are better agriculturists, and inferior huntsman to the Indians, and are violently opposed to leaving the country. If the Indians are permitted to convert them into specie, one great obstacle in the way of removal may be overcome.

I have, therefore, to request that Robert W. W. Williams, and William Baily, may be authorized, under the approval of the agent, to make a purchase of *one hundred and fifty of these negroes.*

"I shall be greatly obliged by having the permission sought for, forwarded to me at Tallahassee, for which place I set out to-morrow.

"Very respectfully,

"Your obedient servant,

"R. K. CALL.[40]

"To the PRESIDENT *of the United States.*"

Endorsement of the President.—"There can be no reason for not giving a permission to purchase their slaves, as it appears to me, directing the agent to see that they obtain a fair price for them.   A.J."

The agent having been requested to superintend the bargaining for these slaves, respectfully remonstrated against the

---

[*] Does General Call only *suppose* they belong to the Indians? If so, he surely would not wish either himself or friends to have possession of property by purchase, the claim to which was likely to be contested;—and surely he would not hold another man's goods or property knowing it to be stolen?

permission or authority granted by the President, and makes the following reply:

"*Seminole Agency, June 17, 1835.*

"Your letter of the 22d ultimo has been received, and I must, in reply, be permitted to express, very respectfully, my great regret that the Department and myself should differ so widely on a subject which I verily believe so deeply involves principles of humanity, justice, and an enterprise, for the success of which, standing in the relation which I do to the government and these people, I am more responsible, perhaps, than any other person.

"It is your privilege to decide, and my duty to submit. Yet if the Department could be satisfied that the undeniable abhorrence of the negroes in this nation to the idea of being transferred from their present state of ease and comparative freedom, to sugar and cotton plantations, under the control of severe task-masters, had been made to subserve the views of the government, by inducing the negroes to exert their known influence over the Indians, through pledges made to them, accompanied by assurances that the removal west would, more than any thing else, serve to secure the existing relations between them and the Indians; then surely the Department, instead of classing them with the Indian skins and furs, would require a punctilious redemption of those pledges.

The admission into the Seminole nation of Mr. Winslet, the Creek agent, for the purpose of recovering three negroes belonging to Mr. Everett,[41] of Georgia, was certainly very unwise, and showed a lack of prudence that seems almost unpardonable. It is granted too, at a time when the highest state of excitement prevailed on the subject, and in the face of objections urged against the permission sanctioned by the President, and in direct contravention of an article in the treaty which provides for the payment of those claims, by the United States.—And it is also a direct violation of those rights which the United States guaranteed should be held sacred, and which is expressly stipulated in the fourth article of the Camp Moultrie treaty: The words are—"The United States promise to guarantee to the said tribe of Indians peaceable possession of the said district of country herein assigned them, reserving the right of opening through it such road as may be deemed *necessary*, and to *restrain and prevent all white persons whatsoever from hunting, settling or otherwise intruding upon it.*"

The ratification of the treaty on the part of the United States having taken place, and the necessary appropriation having been made, the agent was instructed to convene a general council of the Seminole chiefs, and communicate the information to them, so that they might prepare themselves for emigration. Runners were immediately despatched [*sic*] to the various towns to summon the attendance of the chiefs at as early a day as practicable, when their annuities would also be paid them.—The 21st of October 1834, was the day appointed for their assemblage, at Fort King;[42] but, in consequence of the non-arrival of several leading chiefs, those that were in attendance refused to meet the agent in council until the absentees should arrive; accordingly the meeting was postponed for two days.

I propose to give the deliberations of the assembly somewhat at length, in order to let my readers draw their own inferences as to the probability of the ultimate removal of the

Indians without the application of coercive measures, or that the slightest grounds existed for a belief that they could become so far convinced of their error as to voluntarily change their determination and move of their own accord.

PROCEEDINGS IN COUNCIL.

October 23, 1834.

The Council convened this day at 11 o'clock, A. M.

The *agent* stated to the assembled chiefs that he had two government interpreters; that if they wished another and would select one, he, the agent, would invite him to assist in interpreting. *Abraham* was selected by them.

The *agent* then addressed the council as follows:

"Friends and Brothers: I come from your great father, the President of the United States, with a talk: listen to what I say.

"On the 9th of May, 1832, you entered into a treaty at Payne's Landing. I come from the President to tell you that he has complied with all his promises to you in that treaty that he was bound to do before you move, and that you must prepare to move by the time the cold weather of the winter shall have passed away. I have a proposition to you from your brothers, the chiefs of the western Creek nation, but before I present it to you I will read to you the preamble and the first article of the treaty at Payne's Landing. (That part of the treaty was then read, the treaty at Fort Gibson was read; and the map of the country allotted to the Seminoles was then shown to them and explained.) Having thus shown to you that the country

50

which you have acquired beyond the Mississippi, for this which you have by the treaty of Payne's Landing sold to the United States, lies adjoining your brothers of the west, I will proceed to present to you their proposition.

"Instead of settling in the country alloted [*sic*] to you adjoining to them, in a body by yourselves, they invite you to settle promiscuously among them; but they think all will be more prosperous and happy, and that there will be less strife and contention, if you will, on their invitation, relinquish your right to a separate settlement, and settle promiscuously among them. Such an arrangement will, they think, enable the Muscogee people to become, as they were in the days of other years, a great nation. You alone have the right to decide whether you will accept the invitation or not; it is left, *as it should be, entirely optional with you, and no person but* yourselves *has any right to say you shall* or shall not accede to the proposition. Take this with you when you retire, reflect upon it, and make up your minds for yourselves and people.

"Though the President does not believe that any of his red children here are so dishonest and faithless as to refuse to go, yet a circumstance occurred last year which induced a belief that some person or persons around here had a disposition to meddle in regard to the removal—that some person had recommended that a delegation should be sent to the President. This made the President angry.

"The next question arises out of the fifth article of the treaty at Payne's Landing. (That article was read and explained.) The question is, whether those among you who own cattle, (which are to be given up to the United States at a fair valuation,) will prefer to take cattle at your new home, or there receive the amount of money which shall be adjudged to be the value of the cattle you gave up here? I wish those of you who desire cattle to be returned to you at your new homes, for such as you may leave here, to inform me of your wish that the government may be apprised in time to comply.

"The next question is, whether you will petition to go by water, as the best mode of getting all the old men, women, the children, lame, sick, and lazy of your people comfortably along on their journey to their new home?

"The next and last question is, how will you have the next annuity paid to you—will you have it in goods or in money? Should you prefer to receive it in such goods as will suit your wants, your father, the President, will have them delivered to you at fair prices, and much lower than you obtain them from the traders. In conclusion, as your friend and brother, I have only to say, that Captain Russell[43] and myself are to accompany you to your new home; and for myself, and I will add for Captain Russell, who hears me, we pledge ourselves to be your friends; to share your toils and hardships, and your sufferings, if, unfortunately, any of you should unexpectedly suffer."

"The proposition which I present for your decision is:

"1st. Will you accept the invitation of your brothers of the western Creek nation?

"2d. Do you prefer cattle or money, when you arrive t [sic] your new home, for the cattle, which, under the treaty, you must give up here?

"3d. Will you petition to go by water, or do you prefer to go by land?

"4th. How will you have your next annuity paid to you, in money or in goods?

"These are the questions I wish you to deliberate upon, and give me your answer to them as soon as you have made up your minds. When you retire and enter into private council, upon the propositions which I have thus submitted, should you want any further explanations on either point, send for me, I will attend you, give the desired explanation, and retire immediately, so as not to be an intruder on your private council. You are at liberty to retire."

A speaker of the nation, *Holata Amathla,* said they would retire and hold a private council this evening, and also again in the morning; and, after that, they would attend the agent in council. He then addressed the Indian assembly as follows:—

"My Brothers! We have now heard the talk that our father at Washington has sent to us. He says that we made a treaty at Payne's Landing, and we have no excuse now for not doing what we promised. We must be honest. Let us go, my brothers, and talk it over, and don't let us act like fools."

(Reported confidentially.)

At 4 o'clock, P. M., the private Indians met in their camp with their chiefs, when Assiola got up and addressed them:

"My Brothers! The white people got some of our chiefs to sign a paper to give our lands to them, but our chiefs did not do as we told them to do; they done wrong; we must do right.

The agent tells us we must go away from the lands which we live on—our homes, and the graves of our Fathers, and go over the big river among the bad Indians. When the agent tells me to go from my home, I hate him, because I love my home, and will not go from it.

"My Brothers! When the great spirit tells me to go with the white man, I go: but he tells me not to go.—The white man says I shall go, and he will send people to make me go; but I have a rifle, and I have some powder and some lead. I say, we must not leave our homes and lands. If any of our people want to go west we won't let them; and I tell them they are our enemies, and we will treat them so, for the great spirit will protect us."

After a short silence in the council, Holata Amathla was called upon to express his opinions, when he said:

"My Brothers and Friends! You want to hear my talk. When we made a treaty at Payne's, some of us said if the land was good for us, we would go across the great Mississippi. We were told, it would be better for the red people and the red people could be happy there; that if we staid [sic] here the bad white men would wrong us; so we went to see the land our great father said we must have, and it was good land. We told the agents, whom our father sent with us, that we would do as our father bade us. My Brothers! I don't want to talk like a foolish child. My talk is good for my people; and I say we must act honest and do as our great father at Washington tells us."

After Holata Amathla became seated, *Jumper*, the Sense-keeper, was requested to give his views to the Council, which he did as follows:

"My Brothers! You have listened to the talk of our brothers; now hear mine. I do not make talks to-day to break them to-morrow. I told the agent I was glad to see the lands which our great father said we must have, and I told him that I and my people would go, and now we have no excuse. If we don't go, our father will send his men to make us go, and we will lose many of our tribe, because the wrath of the great spirit will come upon us.

"My Brothers! You heard what the agent tells us.—Our father at Washington says we must act like good and honest chiefs, and go without any trouble. Let us show our father that his red children are honest."

Arpiucki then proposed that Holata Amathla should represent to the agent the objections of the nation to a removal; but Holata replied—

"My people! I am not a foolish child to make such a talk; when I talk to the agent, I talk like a man."

Jumper was then selected to speak the sentiments of the nation, the following day.

Friday, October 24, 1834. The Indians again met in council. The agent then told them that he had given them a talk yesterday, and asked them if they were ready to give him an answer to the several propositions which he then referred to them? The first was in regard to the invitation of the western Creeks; the second was on the subject of their cattle; the third was, that if you should wish to go by water, and would say so, I would recommend it to the President; the fourth was, as to whether you will have the next annuity paid to you in money or goods. Upon these points I am now ready to receive your answer.

Abraham was selected as their interpreter.

Holata Mico then rose and said: "God made all of us, and we all came from one woman, sucked one bubby; we hope we shall not quarrel; that we will talk until we get through."

Miconopy then said—"When we were at Camp Moultrie we made a treaty, and we were to be paid our annuity for twenty years. That is all I have got to say."

Jumper said—"At Camp Moultrie they told us all difficulties should be buried for twenty years, from the date of the treaty made there; that after this we held a treaty at Payne's Landing, before the twenty years were out; and they told us we might go and see the country, but that we were not obliged to remove. The land is very good, I saw it, and was glad to see it; the neighbours there are bad people; I do not like them bad Indians, the Pawnees. I went and saw the place; I told the agent that I was a rogue; that he had brought me to the place here along side, and among the rogues, the bad Pawnees, because I am a rogue. I went to see the land, and the commissioners said that the Seminoles must have that land. When we went west to see the land, we had not sold our land here, and we were told only to go and see it.* The Indians there steal horses, and take packs on their horses; they all steal horses

---

* I would again beg leave to refer my readers to the preliminary article to the treaty formed at Payne's Landing, which will fully justify the language here used by *Jumper*. The chief, it will be remembered, was one of the number who were authorized to make an examination of the country west of the Mississippi; but he here confesses that *he* (and consequently the other chiefs) *had no authority to ratify the treaty,* or to contract for the removal of the Seminole nation. He was "*told only to go and see the land,*" and, in conjunction with the other chiefs, to make a report of their mission, and if their description corresponded with that *given to the Seminoles,* by Col. Gadsden, *then* there would be no difficulty on their (the Seminoles') part in closing the bargain. But in corroboration of Jumper's remarks, let us refer

from the different tribes; I do not want to go among such people; your talk seems always good, but we don't feel disposed to go west.

Holata Amathla.—"The horses that were stolen form us by the Cherokees, we never got back (the party that went west.) We then told the agent that the people were bad there; the land was good. When we went there, we saw the Indians bring in scalps to the garrison. When we were there, we had a meeting with M'Intosh; he told us that among all their neighbours they had peace. That he and Col. Arbuckle[44] were to send out to have a treaty of peace with all the Spanish Indians; and when that was done, a report of it was to be sent to Washington. I am sick. I cannot say all I want to say. I am a man that wants to talk coolly and deliberately, and to tell the truth in all things. They promised to send to our nation word when peace was made with all those Indians west of the great river. My brothers! I want the chiefs to address the agent, and express their opinion—as we have different opinions; we will talk it over, and consult, and try to come all of one opinion."

Charley Amathla then rose and said—"The speakers of the nation are all dead; but I recollect some of their words when they had the meeting at Camp Moultrie.[*] I was not there, but heard that we would be at peace, and that we would have our annuity paid to us for twenty years. ⟶ *White people have told me that the treaty of Camp Moultrie, which was made by*

---

to the talk of Charley Amathla.—What does he say?—"*The white people forced us into the treaty.*" And what does Gen. Thompson say, respecting the character of the chief Charley Amathla?—That he was "an intelligent, active and honest chief."

[*] (See page 13.)

great men, and not to be broken, had secured them for twenty years; that seven years of that treaty are still unexpired. I am no half breed, and do not lean on one side. If they tell me to go after the seven years, I say nothing. As to the proposition made us by the agent about removing, I do not say I will not go; but I think that, until the seven years are out, I give no answer. My family I love dearly and sacredly. I do not think it right to take them right off. Our father has often said to me that he loves his children—and they love him. When a man is at home, and got his stock about him, he looks upon it as the subsistence of himself and family. Then when they go off, they reflect and think more seriously, than when quiet at home. I do not complain of the agent's talk. My young men and family are all around me. Should I go west, I should lose many on the path. As to the country west, I looked at it; a weak man cannot get there, the fatigue would be so great; it requires a strong man. I hardly got there. When I went there, the agent, Major Phagan, was a passionate man—he quarrelled [*sic*] with us after we got there. If he had done his duty, it would all have been settled, and there would have been no difficulty. If I know my own heart, I think I am true. If I differ from the agent, he is a free man, and has his right to his talk. I hope his talk will bring all things right, that hereafter we may all live well together. I am pleased with the sight of the agent, and hope we may know each other better."

The *agent* then said—"I have no answer to make to what you have said to me to-day. My talk to you yesterday must

58

and will stand, and you must abide by it. I am surprised at the chiefs, that, after the solemn treaty they entered into at Payne's Landing, they should come to me to-day with such a talk as they have made. Is it any thing like an answer to the propositions and questions which I submitted yesterday, for your consideration and decision? The meeting was appointed for the 21st instant; three days have passed away, and the chiefs come to me to-day with a foolish talk about Camp Moultrie. Is this a talk like chiefs? Is it such as I had a right to expect from you after my honest talk to you? I will not, dare not, receive your talk to-day as any thing like an answer to the questions which I submitted to you yesterday. I must have a direct answer to these questions: The first is, will you accept of the invitation from your brothers of the west? The second is, do you prefer money or cattle, at your new home, for the cattle you will leave here? The third is, do you wish to go by water? The fourth is, do you prefer to have your next annuity paid to you in goods, suitable to your wants, or will you have it in money? And I want, when you meet me again in council, that you give a correct account of the number of your people, that the government may provide for you comfortably while on your journey, whether by land or by water. Now retire, and take as much time as is necessary to deliberate on the points which I have submitted to you; and when you are ready to meet me, let me know. When you come here again, come prepared to act like chiefs, and honourable men; don't bring to me any more foolish talks. Men do not listen to the talks of a child; and remember that the talk I gave you must and will stand.

October 25, 1834. The council convened at 11 o'clock. Interpreters as yesterday.

The *agent* said to the council, "I am ready to receive your answers to the questions which I submitted to you."

Holata Mico.—I have only to repeat what I said yesterday, and to say that the twenty years from the treaty at Moultrie has not yet expired. I never gave my consent to go west; the whites may say so, but I never gave my consent.

Jumper.—We are not satisfied to go until the end of the twenty years, according to the treaty at Camp Moultrie. We were called upon to go to the west, beyond the Mississippi. It is a good country; this is a poor country, we know. We had a good deal of trouble to get there; what would it be for all our tribe?

Miconopy.—"I say, what I said yesterday, I did not sign the treaty."

Agent.—"Abraham, tell Miconopy that I say *he lies*; he did sign the treaty for here is his name."

Charley Amathla.—"The agent told us yesterday we did not talk to the point. I have nothing to say different from what I said yesterday. At Payne's Landing, the *white people forced us into the treaty.* I was there. I agreed to go west and did go west. I went in a vessel, and it made me sick. I undertook to go there; and think that, for so many people, it would be very bad. The Indians and the whites have spilt no blood. They stole things from each other. At Payne's Landing the toma-hawk was buried, and peace was to prevail as long as agreed on between whites and Indians. They agreed at Payne's Land-ing, that if blood was seen in the path to think it was because a person had snagged his foot. We wish to hear the agent's views and opinions on the matter.

Agent.—You tell me your wish to hear me upon the subject of your relations with the United States, and you have told me that you want to talk the matter over calmly, and in good humor. I am not mad; I am your friend. I feel here that I am, and that it is my official duty to be so. All the reply required of me, officially, to your foolish and unreasonable talk, is, that it is no answer to the questions I submitted to you. I cannot, I dare not receive it as an answer. I have told you that you must stand to your bargain. My talk is still the same. You must go west. Your father, the President, who is your friend, will compel you to go. Therefore, be not deluded by any hope or expectation that you will be permitted to remain here. You have expressed a wish to hear my views and opinion upon the whole matter. As a man, and your friend, I will this day deign to reason with you; for I want to show you that your talk of to-day is the foolish talk of a child. Holata Mico tells me that one God made us all, and that we all descended from one woman, and drew nourishment from one breast. When I admit this truth, as I cheerfully do, I feel here in my bosom that you are my brothers, and that I am your friend. We should therefore act towards each other as brothers, and not speak with a forked tongue; if we do, or if we try to break our solemn talks, that Great Spirit that made us will punish us. Miconopy tells me that he did not sign the treaty at Payne's Landing, and that the twenty years of the annuity, according to the Camp Moultrie treaty, is not expired. I hold in my hand the twenty at Payne's Landing; here is Miconopy's name and mark to it;

it was witnessed by (here the witnesses were named.) They are honest men, therefore Miconopy does not tell the truth. He did sign the treaty at Payne's Landing.

Miconopy here interrupted the agent by saying—"I did not touch the pen; I only reached over (the body of another chief) and pointed at it."

Agent.—"You *lie*, for you did touch the pen: you attempted to sign by pointing, but you were told to touch it. John Hicks (the chief) bent down out of your way. You did sign the treaty."

The agent resumes his address to the council—"Jumper says, they agreed at Payne's Landing to go and examine the country west, but they were not bound to remove to it until the nation should agree to do so, after the return of the delegation; and he adds, what others of you have said, that the treaty of Camp Moultrie was to stand for twenty years. Such a talk from Jumper surprises me, for he is a man of sense. He understands the treaty at Payne's Landing, which he signed; he was the first named in that treaty, of the delegation appointed to go west; he knows that that treaty gave him and the other members of the delegation authority to decide whether the nation should remove or not. (I am surprised at these remarks of General Thompson, when by a reference to the treaty which he then held in his hand, he would have seen in black and white that *they were not authorised* to contract for the removal of the nation.—W. P.) He visited and examined the country that was proposed to you, and he, with all the other members of the delegation, decided that the country is good; that the Seminole nation should remove to it according to the treaty at Payne's Landing. The Indian Board of Commissioners made a treaty with your brothers of the west, by which they agreed to re-unite with you, and Jumper, with all the other members of the delegation, made a final treaty which I now hold in my hand, with all their names subscribed to it, confirming the treaty at Payne's Landing. The President therefore will be astonished when he hears that Jumper has made a different talk now. Charley Amathla says that the treaty at Camp Moultrie was made by men, and that it has seven years to stand, and that they were not bound by the treaty of Payne's Landing to re-move west, because the question was not submitted to the Seminole nation after their delegation returned, whether they were willing to go. You all say that, as there are seven years of the twenty years' annuity stipulated in the treaty of Camp Moultrie, yet to run, you are not bound to go until the full time is expired; and yet the whole of you signed a treaty at Payne's Landing, by which you solemnly bound yourselves to remove within three years from the ratification of that treaty, and the whole of the delegation that went west confirmed that promise by entering into a final agreement to do so, by which the whole nation is bound. You know you had the right to make that treaty; you did make it, and you know and feel that you are bound by it. But you say the treaty at Camp Moultrie was made by men, thereby indicating that the treaty at Payne's Landing was not made by men. Was it made by old women and children? If the spirit of Hicks is now flitting around us, how must he grieve at your conduct; how blush to hear you acknowledge you are not men; that you are unfit to be chiefs. But it is said by Charley Amathla, that the white people forced you into the treaty at Payne's Landing. If you were so cowardly as to be forced by any body to do what you ought not to do, you are unfit to be chiefs, and your people ought to hurl you from your stations. But you know that this is not the truth; you know you were not forced to do it. According to the form of the white people's government, each state and territory has its own boundaries. The states have the right to extend their laws over the Indians located within their respective limits. With the permission of Congress, the territories may do the same: Georgia, Alabama, and other states, have already extended their jurisdiction over the Indians within their respective limits. The Creeks, Choctaws, Chickasaws and Cherokees, who live in the states, are moving west of the Mississippi river, because they cannot live under the white people's laws; they are gone and going, and the Seminole nation are a small handful to their number. Two governments cannot exist in the same boundary of territory. Where Indians remain within the limits of a state or territory until the jurisdiction of a state or territory shall be extended over them, the Indian government, laws, and chiefships, are forever done away—the Indians are subject to the white man's law. The Indian must be tried, whether for debt or crime, in the white man's court; the Indian's law is not to be known there; the Indian's evidence is not to be admitted there; the Indian will, in every thing, be subject to the control of the white man. It is this view of the subject which induces your father, the President, to settle his red children beyond the limits of the states and territories where the white man's law is never to reach you, and where you and your children are to possess the land, while the grass grows and the water runs. He feels for his red children as a father should feel. It is therefore that he made the treaty with you at Payne's Landing, and for the same reason he will compel you to comply with your bargain. But let us look a little more closely into your own situation. Suppose (what is however impossible) that you could be permitted to remain here a few years longer, what would be your condition? This land will soon be surveyed, sold to, and settled by, the whites. There is now a surveyor in the country; the jurisdiction of the territory will soon be extended over this country. Your laws will be set aside, your chiefs will cease to be chiefs; claims for debt and for your negroes would be set up against you by bad white men, or you would perhaps be charged with crimes affecting life; you would be hailed before the white man's court; the claims against you for debt, for your negroes, or other property, and the charges of crime preferred against you, would be decided by the white man's law. White men would be witnesses against you; Indians would not be permitted to give evidence; your condition, in a very few years, would be hopeless wretchedness.* Thus, you may see, that were it possible for you to remain here a few years longer, you

---

* What a palpable violation of the third article in the treaty at Camp Moultrie, would the United States have committed by permitting such infringements upon the rights of these red men of the forest, who they had sacredly pledged themselves to protect and guard form injury! Can it be imagined that Gen. Thompson could believe that these flagrant acts of injustice and fraud would have been perpetrated, in defiance of the protection of the United States? Or, did he merely make use of these *bug-a-boos* to frighten the Indians? *Oh, tempora, oh mores!* How degraded must we be when we prove faithless to our obligations with weaker powers! The words of the third article in the Camp Moultrie, run thus:

"The United States will take the Florida Indians under their care and patronage, *and will afford them protection against all persons whatsoever."*

would be reduced to hopeless poverty, and when urged by hunger to ask, perhaps, of the man who thus would have ruined you, (and is perhaps now tampering with you for the purpose of getting your property,) for a crust of bread, you must be called an Indian dog, and be ordered to clear out. (Here *Assiola,* was seated by Miconopy, urged him to be firm in his resolution.) Your father, the President, sees all these evils, and will save you from them by removing you west; and I stand up for the last time to tell you, that you must go; and if not willingly, you will be compelled to go. I should have told you that no more annuity will be paid to you here. (*Assiola* replied, that he did not care whether any more was ever paid.) I hope you will, on more mature reflection, act like honest men, and not compel me to report you to your father, the President, as faithless to your engagements.

Assiola said, the decision of the chiefs was given—that they did not intend to give any other answer.

Miconopy said—"I do not intend to remove."

The Agent.—"I am now fully satisfied that you are wilfully [*sic*] disposed to be entirely dishonest in regard to your engagements with the President, and regret that I must so report you. The talk which I have made to you must and will stand. Retire and prepare your sticks to receive your annuity tomorrow.[" *sic*]

It is scarcely necessary to call attention to the remarks of General Thompson in reply to the Chiefs, (see page 51,) as the *mockery* conveyed therein must naturally attract the reader's eye. General Thompson says, with much truth and justice on his side, that "no person has a right to say you (the Seminoles) shall go," or that "you shall accede to the proposition" made to you by the Creek nation, but "it is left, as it should be, entirely

REMARKS ON THE FOREGOING.

General Thompson, in speaking of the results of this council says—"They then requested that I, as their agent and friend, would give them my views and opinions upon the subject of their relations with the United States. In com-

---

optional with you." Immediately after expressing these sentiments in council, he makes the following remark to one of the chiefs: "The President, backed by the Secretary of War and the whole Congress, never should compel me to act so dishonourably *as to violate the treaty made with your people.* If such a thing was required of me, I would spurn the President's commission and retire to the bosom of my family." General Thompson hereby acknowledges that they were guaranteed a separate tract of land in the Creek country, and it was entirely optional with them whether they should go and amalgamate with the Creek Indians or not; and the inference therefore is, that the United States had no right to force the Seminoles to settle promiscuously among the Creeks. But has not the government made an effort to enforce the project?—Yes! And has not General Thompson used every exertion to carry the instructions of his government into effect?—No one can deny it. Therefore, I say that, on the subject connected with removal, the professions of the agent have illy accorded with the principles which he has practised. In other words, General Thompson has indubitably adhered to government orders, and endeavoured to execute them, even in opposition to his own avowed sentiments of honour, justice and truth.

Charley Amathla was one of the chiefs that went on the exploring mission; and, on page 58, the reader will find the following words—"The agent, Major Phagan, was a passionate man, and he quarrelled [*sic*] with us after we got there. If the agent had done his duty all would have been settled and there would be no difficulty." Now read the following last clause in the agreement made at Fort Gibson, on the 28th of March, between the commissioners on the part of the United States and the Seminole delegation: "The said Seminole chiefs *having expressed high confidence in the friendship and integrity of their present agent, Major Phagan, respectfully request that he may be appointed their future agent in the west."* Who can believe that the delegation *voluntarily* appended their names to this instrument, with a full understanding of its meaning? Or will it be believed, that the Indians could have so much dissembled as to cloak their hatred to this man, and to seem what they were not, for the purpose of sacrificing him at a future day? I am reluctantly compelled to hazard the opinion that they were, indeed, *forced into the measure.*

pliance with which, I gave in substance what you have in my second talk herewith enclosed. During the delivery of my second talk, I was frequently interrupted by some of the chiefs, especially a leading chief,[*] who was a member of the exploring delegation, a circumstance so unusual in an Indian council as to satisfy me that they were not only afraid that I would produce a proper impression on their minds of the Indians, but that they are obstinately fixed in a resolution to disregard the treaty of Payne's Landing. While I was portraying to them the utter and inevitable ruin which would overwhelm them, were it possible for them to remain in their present location a few years longer, silence ensued their previous frequent interruptions; they were awe-struck by the picture I presented to them of utter desolation and hopeless wretchedness, and their minds, especially Miconopy's, (whom the Indians look to as a principal chief,) seemed engrossed and deeply interested. At that important crisis I heard Powel [Osceola], a bold and dashing young chief, who was seated by Miconopy, and who is vehemently opposed to the removal of the Indians, speak to the latter, apparently in much earnestness, and the interpreter informed me, subsequently, that Powel then urged Miconopy to be firm in his resolution. Holata Amathla, one of the principal chiefs, displayed a magnanimity of character and a nobleness of soul meriting a better fate than that which I fear awaits him; he was in very bad health,—said but little; but that little was a bold and manly declaration of his determination to adhere, in good faith, to his engagements with the United States, and it was coupled with a reproof on those who evinced a disposition to prove faithless. Holata Amathla and Fucta Lusta Hadjo, one of his confidential chiefs, are of opin-

---

[*] Coa Hajo (Alligator.)

ion that their own people and party embrace about one-third of the nation. These two chiefs informed me secretly that their lives were threatened; that they believed themselves and families, with some of their people, are in danger; and they appealed to me for the protection which would be afforded to them by permission to visit their friends on the Appalachicola river, under express stipulations that they will promptly return to the Seminole country, or join the Indians on their emigrating journey, when called on by me. This protection I have, on mature deliberation, determined to afford them, when it shall become obviously necessary, but I directed Holata Emartla to be on the look out, stay as long as he can with safety, as I confidently expect that the government will soon enable me to protect him and his people here, which he seemed delighted to hear.

"A full view of all the circumstances, leaves me without doubt that these deluded people have determined to resist the execution of the treaty of Payne's Landing.

"Having thus given you a full view of the existing state of things here, I feel it an imperious duty to urge the necessity of a *strong* reinforcement of this post,[*] (Fort King,) and the location of a *strong* force at Tampa Bay, as early as possible. An imposing force, thus promptly marshalled to coerce these refractory people, will have the effect to crush the hopes of those who have been tampering with them; awe the chiefs into a proper respect for the government; afford protection to the neighbouring white settlements; and supersede the necessity of Holata Amathla and his followers fleeing the country."

---

[*] There was at this period at the two posts *two hundred and thirty-five men.*

69

In a letter, dated about one month after this council had dispersed, General Thompson says,—"I have drawn the reins of government close about them. They will, however, not remove, but as forced to do so. I am more confirmed every day in the opinion that they have been tampered with by designing, unprincipled white men; and they have come to the conclusion, that by obstinately persisting in their claim to the right to remain here until the expiration of twenty years, from the date of the treaty at Camp Moultrie, and abstaining from the commission of any outrage, their claim will be finally acquiesced in by the government; and I have been informed, by confidential persons among them, that *they laugh at the idea of the little handful of men at this post being able to compel them to remove.*"

Governor Duval also writes to the Secretary of War, and says,—"If it is the intention of the government to remove, under the late treaty, a part of the Florida Indians, I would suggest the *advantage of ordering a respectable military force,* for a time, to Cantonment Brook [Ft. Brooke], at Tampa Bay. With *every* precaution and *assistance of the Department,* the superintendant and agent will have *much difficulty in carrying the treaty into effect.* The traders (not licensed) are constantly interfering with the objects and views of the government, using every art to alarm the Indians, and deter them from emigrating."

And in a subsequent communication Thompson says, (27th January, 1835)—"With this report of myself to you for duty, permit me to suggest that the *military force*, stationed in and on the border of this nation, *is not large enough* to effect the object for which it was intended.

"The command at Fort King and at Tampa Bay is frittered down to a mere handful, by details of parties to patrol the country adjacent to the Indian boundary, to drive the Indians and keep them within their limits, and commands to guard suspected trading houses near the Indian border."

General Clinch also recommends an increase of military force; and the Secretary of War in reply, says—"I have submitted to the President your proposition for the employment of a mounted military force; but under existing circumstances there is no necessity for the measure." And, at a subsequent period, Lieutenant Harris,[45] the disbursing agent, says,—"The time fixed for assembling these Indians for removal, is the 8th January, 1836. It is necessary that prompt and efficient measures should be adopted to accomplish this object; among which are *an increase of military force at Fort King.*"

And what says General Eaton on the same subject:—"You will want such an imposing force as to overawe resistance. The few companies you have ordered, will not produce this result. They will serve but to begin the fight, and to awaken angry feelings, so that in the sequel the militia will have to be called, which will end in the butchery of these miserable people. *Send a strong, imposing, regular force,* which can be commanded. Send only a handful of men, and difficulties will come upon you."

Having now adduced sufficient evidence of the difficulties which existed as early as October 1834, on the subject of emigration, I leave the public to draw their own conclusions; and I would respectfully ask them, whether in their estimation the

71

agents of the War Department have properly executed those important trusts which were confided to them.

At the time when these suggestions were made to the Department, the whole force employed in Florida amounted to about *two hundred and fifty* men, more than one-half of whom were at Fort Brooke, one hundred miles from the agency. Can it then be wondered at, that the Indians should "laugh at the idea of this little handful of men being able" to awe them into submission?—Why were nearly three thousand government soldiers suffered to remain, inactive, at Fort Pike, Fortress Monroe, Fort Pickens, Fort Morgan, Fort Wood, Fort Washington, Fort Severn, Fort Macon, Fort Johnson, at New Orleans, Savannah and elsewhere, when their services were so imperiously required in Florida? Can it be doubted that the presence of a respectable military force at this—the proper period—would have saved the millions of property which have been destroyed—the mass of blood which has been spilled—and, furthermore, the *five millions of dollars which this war will cost*? Therefore, is not the War Department highly culpable in neglecting to conform to these important suggestions; and can they be justified, under any circumstances short of the actual existence of hostilities, and the requirement of these troops in another quarter?

The appointment of General Wiley Thompson as agent for the Seminole Indians, was made in November 1833, in place of Major Phagan, who was dismissed in consequence of his numerous frauds upon the Indians. Several fatal rencontres [*sic*] had taken place about this period and in the early part of 1834, all of which were clearly traced to the effects of intemperance. Two negroes belonging to General Clinch were forcibly seized by the intoxicated Indians, and while endeavouring to effect their escape, they received such severe injuries as to cause their death almost immediately. General Thompson writes to the commissioner of Indian affairs:—"My personal safety has been more than once endangered by the intoxication of Indians, and I consider myself no more safe from the proprietors of the numerous dirty little whiskey *doggeries,* located around the Indian borders, on whom I have been as severe as I have power to be. I have been so provoked, as to be almost tempted to order the chiefs to demolish the little log huts and rude shantees hovering upon the Indian border, in which the *Indian's bane* is kept for sale."

Early after this, he submitted a *project* to the Legislative Council of Florida for suppressing the sale of spirituous liquors to the Indians, in the hope that, by excluding the traders in that article from the nation, it would effectually prevent the improper influence which it was known they exerted over the Indians to excite them against emigration. But to render this law effective in its operation, it could not but have been foreseen, would require the aid of a considerable military force, as the numerous extensive swamps, marshes, hammocks, bays, rivers, creeks and inlets, with which the country abounds, so aptly adapted to favour clandestine traffic, affords a very sufficient security to those who may be disposed to disregard the law: and I therefore think that, under these circumstances, the project was both impolitic and unwise; for, while the difficulty in obtaining it served but to inflame the already hostile feelings of part of the tribe, it engendered dissatisfaction among those who probably might have been induced to comply with the treaty. Yet while we view this step as one of doubtful policy—considering the time it was introduced, the location of the country, the absence of efficient military aid, and the exasperated feelings of the Indians—we must admit that, if differently circumstanced, the pure and philanthropical intentions of General Thompson would have been attended with the happiest consequences. In a letter to the Department, General Thompson remarks—"It could not have escaped observation, that the Indians, after they had received their annuity, purchased an unusually large quantity of powder and lead. I saw one keg of powder carried off by one chief, and I am informed that several whole kegs were purchased. I did not forbid the sale of those articles to the Indians, because, as such a course would have been a declaration of my apprehensions, it might produce a sudden and immediate eruption. It may be proper to add, that I was heretofore informed that the chiefs have a deposit of forty or fifty kegs of powder, which I did not credit at the time." And in a subsequent letter, *written nearly six months afterwards,* he says—"For the purpose of reducing the refractory Indians to a sense of dependence, and to withhold from them the means of doing mischief, I have prohibited the sale of *powder, lead* and *arms.*

This notion of the General's is, to me inexplicable. He considers it would have had a dangerous tendency to prohibit the sale of the "means of doing mischief," when it was at least presumable their supplies were limited; allows them to be supplied by the traders, notwithstanding this ominous circumstance, for a period of six months longer—and when they had amply prepared themselves for an able resistance, and required

74

no further supplies, he suppresses the sale of those means of doing mischief, apparently under the conviction that so far from its being *then* viewed 'as a declaration of his apprehensions,' it would evince a regardlessness of any resistance they might attempt to make. Is it not a remarkable oversight of the General's, in permitting the further sale of ammunition to them, when he discovered that they were investing their annuities in that manner? Why wait until the restriction was no longer necessary—until they had supplied their wants? Was not the order enforced at a most unfortunate period—when it only proved a source of additional irritation? It is true, it continued but a short time in operation, as the President foresaw the evil consequences which would flow from it, and he directed its immediate repeal.

"I was informed," says General Thompson, "*that it has been usual* to make presents to the Indians during the payment of the annuity. I did not feel myself *authorized* to pursue the custom, and therefore declined doing so." Here is another unfortunate error of the General's, in withholding from the poor Indian those little presents which custom had taught him to look for—which, from our earliest intercourse with them, has been in practice, and considered by him a token of our friendship and peace. Hence a departure from that custom, under the existing state of things, seemed to have evinced a total disregard of their friendly feelings, and no doubt contributed much to that intense hatred of him, which the Indians, on several occasions, openly manifested.

In the administration of General Thompson, (no doubt through a mistaken zeal for the Indian,) various acts of injustice were practised which have materially affected the cause of removal. Indians have been deprived of liquor whenever found in their possession, and in instances where it should have been held as sacredly inviolable as that belonging to the white man; though I am yet to learn, if in *any* case we can with justice observe one principle of law in relation to the latter, and practise another in our intercourse with the Indian. The laws which were established for the suppression of illicit trade with the Indians, applied in its construction to the *venders,* or distributors of liquor *alone,* and *not* to the purchaser; therefore, after the trade was effected, and the Indian had given an equivalent for the article, no power could righteously dispossess him of it. Numerous instances have occurred in which General Thompson gave orders to take liquor from them, and, on one occasion, I am told, he ordered a quantity taken from Assiola, (Powell.) The sub-chief became very much exasperated, and (I was informed that this was the occasion referred to when Thompson ordered him to be placed in chains and kept within the fort) he afterwards remarked in the presence of an interpreter, *"that man shall suffer for this, but the time is not come."* It was deemed unnecessary to communicate the threat of the Indian to the General, but alas! how true have his words been proved!

The period for the removal of the Big Swamp Indians having passed by, in consequence of the non-acknowledgment of the treaty on the part of the United States, and as they had been previously informed that they would be called on to remove at the appointed time, they of course did not plant that season, and consequently became very destitute of food: the preceding season having been unpropitious for the production of their crops, those who did plant had barely sufficient for their own subsistence; and the Big Swamp Indians were therefore thrown upon the charity of others for their support. No orders having been granted by the government, the agent did not feel authorized to distribute provisions among them, so that the Big Swamp inhabitants saw but a wretched existence before their eyes; and as stern necessity knows no law, pillaging became the order of the day. Discovering the evil which this course of things was calculated to produce, the agents strongly recommended the government to permit the distribution of some corn which was then on hand, until their crops could be gathered in; and it was hoped that this display of liberality on the part of the United States would make them sensible of the good will entertained for them, and perhaps establish a better feeling on the subject of emigration. In a few weeks the consent of the authorities was had, and accordingly about 800 bushels of corn were distributed among those who were really destitute; but this bribe failed to have the desired effect, as the question of removal was based upon the principle of property or no property: for, to locate themselves among the Creeks, it was evident to them that they would be divested of their principal means of wealth, and their degradation would then be inevitable.

Another effort was made to obtain the general consent of the nation, and they were therefore requested to assemble in council for the purpose of listening to the last talk that their father, the President, would make to them on this side of the Mississippi river. The talk had been delivered to several of the chiefs, and about one hundred and fifty of their people; but as Jumper remarked, that, on a question of such vast importance, and affecting so deeply the interest of all, the chiefs then present considered the nation so feebly represented that they could give no answer to the proposition of the agent, until a more general council could be summoned. Accordingly, at the solicitation of Jumper, thirty days were granted them for a collection of the chiefs and warriors, and, on the 22d of April, 1835, several hundred met in council.

The business of the convention having been opened, General Thompson expressed his hopes that they had assembled to fulfil [*sic*] their promise, and to act like honest men. The treaty of Payne's Landing was read and explained to them, and the following talk of President Jackson was then delivered.

"To the Chiefs and Warriors of the Seminole Indians in Florida.

"MY CHILDREN: I am sorry to have heard that you have been listening to bad counsels. You know me, and you know that I would not deceive, nor advise you to do any thing that was unjust or injurious. Open your ears and attend to what I shall now say to you. They are the words of a friend, and the words of truth.

"The white people are settling around you. The game has disappeared from your country. Your people are poor and hungry. All this you have perceived for some time. And nearly three years ago, you made an agreement with your friend, Colonel Gadsden, acting on the part of the United States, by which you agreed to cede your lands in Florida, and to remove and join your brothers, the Creeks, in the country west of the Mississippi. You annexed a condition to this agreement, that certain chiefs, named therein, in whom you placed confidence, should proceed to the western country, and examine whether it was suitable to your wants and habits; and whether the Creeks residing there were willing to permit you to unite with them as one people; and if the persons thus sent, were satisfied on these heads, then the agreement made with Colonel Gadsden was to be in full force.

"In conformity with these provisions, the chiefs named by you, proceeded to that country, and having examined it, and having become satisfied respecting its character and the favourable disposition of the Creeks, they entered into an agreement with commissioners on the part of the United States, by which they signified their satisfaction on these subjects, and finally ratified the agreement made with Colonel Gadsden.

"I now learn that you refuse to carry into effect the solemn promises thus made by you, and that you have stated to the officers of the United States, sent among you, that you will not remove to the western country.

"MY CHILDREN: I have never deceived, nor will I ever deceive, any of the red people. I tell you that you must go, and that you will go. Even if you had a right to stay, how could you live where you now are? You have sold all your country. You have not a piece as large as a blanket to sit down upon. What is to support yourselves, your women and children? The tract you have ceded will soon be surveyed and sold, and immediately afterwards will be occupied by a white population.

You will soon be in a state of starvation. You will commit depredations upon the property of our citizens. You will be resisted, punished, perhaps killed. Now, is it not better peaceably to remove to a fine, fertile country, occupied by your own kindred, and where you can raise all the necessaries of life, and where game is yet abundant? The annuities payable to you, and the other stipulations made in your favour, will make your situation comfortable, and will enable you to increase and improve. If, therefore, you had a right to stay where you now are, still every true friend would advise you to remove. But you have no right to stay, and you must go. I am very desirous that you should go peaceably and voluntarily. You shall be comfortably taken care of and kindly treated on the road, and when you arrive in your new country, provisions will be issued to you for a year, so that you can have ample time to provide for your future support.

"But lest some of your rash young men should forcibly oppose your arrangements for removal, I have ordered a large military force to be sent among you. I have directed the commanding officer, and likewise the agent, your friend, General Thompson, that every reasonable indulgence be held out to you. But I have also directed that one-third of your people, as provided for in the treaty, be removed during the present season. If you listen to the voice of friendship and truth, you will go quietly and voluntarily. But should you listen to the bad birds that are always flying about you, and refuse to remove, I have then directed the commanding officer to remove you by force. This will be done. I pray the Great Spirit, therefore, to incline you to do what is right.

> "Your friend,
>
> "A. JACKSON.

"*Washington, February* 16, 1835."

The reading of this talk having been enforced with such observations as were deemed necessary by Gen. Thompson, he requested them to retire and consult among themselves, and then to give him their final decision upon the subject.

In a short time the chiefs signified their desire to be heard, when Jumper arose and expressed sentiments opposed to the treaty and to a removal from their present homes; yet, sentiments solicitous of our friendship, and averse to a hostile resistance should we employ force to oblige them to go.

He was followed in turn by Miconopy, Charley Amathla, Arpiucki, Coa Hajo, Holata Mico, Moke Is She Larni, Tustenuggee, and others, who advocated his views with more or less power; and as the day was wasting and the Indians were not disposed to listen to the agent's entreaties for a voluntary removal, General Clinch arose and briefly, yet firmly, declared to the chiefs "that the time of expostulation had passed; that already too much had been said, and nothing had been done; that the influence of the agents of government, their powers of pursuasion [*sic*] and of argument had been exhausted, both in public councils and in private interviews, to induce them to do right; that we had lingered long enough in the performance of our duties to have averted, had they been willing, the evils which threatened their foolish resistance to the fulfillment of pledges solemnly and fairly made by them,

and that now it was time to *act*. He had been sent here to enforce the treaty; he had warriors enough to do it, and he would
do it. It was the question now whether they would go of their
own accord, or go by force?"

The General, agent and officers then left them, with the in-
junction that the following day must find them all of one opinion on the removal question, or he would apply force in bringing the refractory to submission.

The firmest friend to emigration was Fucta Lusta Hajo
(Black dirt.) In consequence of sickness he did not arrive in
time for the council of the first day, but he heard from Generals Thompson and Clinch that the friendly chiefs were too timid in the expression of their opinions, and he then said that he
had come for the express purpose of speaking his mind fully
on the subject, and if he should lose his life for doing his duty,
he had but one to lose, and that should be sacrificed in the
cause.

On the morrow, the 23d., the chiefs and warriors again
convened in council, and sent word to the agent that they were
ready to talk with him. On his arrival at the council, General
Thompson discovered that Miconopy was absent, and, on inquiry, he was informed that the chief was sick—that he had a
pain in the stomach; but the agent viewed this as a shuffling
trick, and that his object was to shun responsibility. Jumper
was again speaker, and when asked the result of their deliberations, similar replies to the preceding day were made. After
several of the leading chiefs had spoken, the veteran Fucta
Lusta Hajo, (or Black dirt,) then arose, and in the firmest and
most decisive manner denounced all who opposed the execution of the treaty, and that if they were his brethren and wished

him so to value them, they must act consistently with the wishes of their great father. He said the good of his people was his only study, and that what was their interest, was his also; he signed the treaty, because others signed it, and having done so he would unflinchingly act up to it. During this speech of Fucta Lusta Hajo, he was frequently interrupted by several of those who were opposed to him, but he bravely and fearlessly delivered his talk without regarding or replying to them. When he had finished, General Thompson then placed on a table in front of the chiefs, the following agreement, and requested such as were willing to remove voluntarily to come forward and sign it. It was in these words:—"We, the under-signed chiefs and sub-chiefs of the Seminole tribe of Indians, do hereby, for ourselves and for our people, voluntarily acknowledge the validity of the treaty between the United States and the Seminole nation, made and concluded at Payne's Landing, on the Ocklawaha river, on the 9th of May 1832, and the treaty between the United States and the Semi-nole nation, made and concluded at Fort Gibson, on the 28th day of March 1833, by Montford Stokes, H. L. Ellsworth and J. F. Schermerhorn, commissioners on the part of the United States, and the delegates of the said nation of Seminole Indi-ans on the part of said nation; and we, the said chiefs and sub-chiefs, do for ourselves and for our people, freely and fully assent to the above-recited treaties in all their provisions and stipulations. Done in Council at the Seminole Agency, this 23d day of April, 1835."

In consequence of the bold and manly declaration of the

chief Fucta Lusta Hajo, eight of the principal chiefs of the nation and eight sub-chiefs advanced and signed the article. Five of the principal chiefs remained opposed, viz., Miconopy, Jumper, Holata Mico, Coa Hajo and Arpiucki. The former chief, as before mentioned, was absent, and as the agent knew that Miconopy controlled the movements of many of them, he demanded of Jumper whether Miconopy "intended to abide by the treaty or not?" And when Jumper finally confessed that he was *authorized* to say that Miconopy *did not*, the agent promptly declared that "he no longer considered Miconopy as chief; that his name should be struck from the council of the nation; that he should treat all who acted like him in the like manner, and that he would neither acknowledge nor do business with him, or with any others as a chief, who did not honestly comply with the terms of his engagements; that the door was, however, still open to them if they wished to act honestly." In consequence of this the *names* of the above *five opposing chiefs were struck from the council of the nation.*

Now the injurious tendency of this act must be obvious to all who will for a moment reflect upon the already disastrous state of things, and "our very delicate relations with these Indians, and that all causeless irritation should be avoided." It must evidently have been looked upon by them as a disgrace and punishment, and therefore excited them to oppose more virulently the project of emigration.

On this subject the Secretary of War remarks—"It is not necessary for me to enter into much detail on the subject presented by you. I understand from Mr. Harris, that he communicated to you the President's views on the subject of the chiefs whom you declined to recognize in all questions connected with the removal of the Seminoles. I understand that the President deemed this course an incorrect one; and it seems to me obviously liable to strong objections. We do not assume the right of determining who shall be the chiefs in the various Indian tribes; this is a matter of internal policy which must necessarily be left to themselves. And if, when we have a grave matter for adjustment with one of the tribes, we undertake to say *it shall be* determined by a particular class of individuals, we certainly should render ourselves obnoxious to censure. It appears to me the proper course, upon important questions, is to treat directly with the tribe itself; and if they depute their chiefs, or any other individual to act for them, we must either recognize such authority or abandon the object in view."

None can disagree with the views therein set forth by Mr. Cass, and none can deny that this step of General Thompson was a high-handed and tyrannical one.

But while on this point, another strikes me as peculiarly analagous [*sic*] to it—I allude the determination of the government that the Seminole Indians *should* (*i. e.* must) go and amalgamate with the Creeks and become as one nation, subject to the same government and laws. In this decision of "the Government" I can discover nothing short of a palpable violation of the very principles which are above laid down by Mr. Secretary Cass.

Early in June 1835, Assiola called at the Seminole agency for the purpose of entering complaint against some white men, who had a few days previous maltreated two of his people. Thompson had, the day before Assiola called, been informed by the whites that the Indians were found outside of their boundary; that a skirmish ensued, and one of the Indians was wounded; and Thompson therefore told Assiola that *his* men were in fault, and that he should make a demand for their delivery to the civil authorities. The Indian, however, contended, that his people had not fired upon the whites, and he accused Thompson of partiality. This somewhat enraged the General and he ordered the chief away; but in return for his stern authority, Assiola passed some severe reflections on him for taking liquor from him on a former occasion. For this Thompson ordered him to be arrested and confined in irons. Four of the soldiers of the garrison were detailed for that duty, and it was with difficulty they succeeded in overcoming him; they secured him about two hundred yards from the fort, amidst a shower of the bitterest imprecations upon Gen. Thompson, which he continued to utter in a perfect state of phrensy [*sic*] for some hours after he was secured. The following morning his anger was somewhat relaxed, and he then sent word to the General that if he would release him he would signify his approbation of the treaty and also induce others to do so. The General refused to set him at liberty unless he would give him security for his future good behaviour, and that he would prove faithful to his pledge. Accordingly Assiola sent for some of the friendly chiefs and solicited their intercession on his behalf; under the most solemn pledge that he would throw no farther obstacles in the way of the agent, and in consideration of his fulfilling the promise, that he would come forward and meet those friendly chiefs in council within five days from that time, and subscribe to the acknowledgement of the treaty, he was released. On the fifth day after he appeared with seventy-nine men, women and children, and redeemed his promise.

On the 11th of August, (Dalton,)[46] the mail carrier between Fort King and Fort Brooke, was met within six miles of the latter place by a party of Micosukees, who seized the reins of his horse, and dragging him from the saddle, shot him. The horribly mangled body was discovered some days afterwards concealed in the woods. General Clinch demanded the surrender of the party who committed the murder, and expresses or runners were despatched [*sic*] to their chiefs, who promised to deliver them over to the civil authorities as soon as possible; but they had sought refuge among the old *Red Sticks* in the neighbourhood of the Ouithlacoochee, and, shielded by them, eluded detection. This murder was effected to satisfy their revenge for the Indian (Fuxe) who was killed in the June preceding by some of Captain Walker's neighbours, and of which previous mention has been made.

It would seem very doubtful from the following proceedings, in a council held at Fort King, whether it was the determination of some of the chiefs, who are now hostile, to persist in their opposition to removal provided they could be so far separated from the influence of the Creek councils as to leave them in the enjoyment of their hereditary possessions; or that the President would allow them a separate agent to watch over their interests and protect them from the encroachments of other tribes. For it is obvious that their greatest objections to leaving Florida have been based upon the liability of losing their slaves, when they should have removed to the new country. In all their councils this subject has been discussed, over and over again, and again reiterated even to the last day: recommendation after recommendation has followed from agents and friends of the government, but these solicitations have been responded to by the cry of *"economy:"* "Economy in the administration of *our* government is the order of the day," and thus the sacred *rights of the Indian* have been bartered away in the endeavours of the government to preserve the vain boasting of "retrenchment and reform."

—"Fruitless are thy efforts—vain appealing
To grasping avarice which ne'er relents—
To party power that shamelessly is stealing,
Banditti like, whatever spoil it scents.
If honour, justice, truth, had not forsaken
The place long hallowed as its bright abode,
The faith of treaties never had been shaken;—
Our country would have kept the trust she owed."

This council was convened on the 19th day of August 1835, at the request of the undernamed chiefs and sub-chiefs, and the talk was delivered in the presence of several of the officers stationed at Fort King.

Holata Amathla,	Yaha Fixico,
Charley Amathla,	Emathlochee,
Fucta Lusta Hajo,	Acola Hajo,
Conhatkee Mico,	Tustinuc Yaha,
Otulkee Amathla,	Powshaila,
Coa Hajo,	Albartu Hajo,
Foshatchee Mico,	Cochattee Fixico,
Tustenuggee Hajo,	Ochee Hajo,
Billy Hicks,	Cheti Haiola,

Assiola,	Cosa Tustenuggee,
Billy John,	Tokosa Fixico,
Cosatchee Amathla,	Conchattee.
Yaha Amathla,	

Holata Amathla was then requested by the chiefs to address the officers, and make known to their great father, through them, the object of their visit; after a short silence, he commenced:—

"My Friends: We have come to see you to talk with you on a subject of great interest to us. We want you to open your ears to us and tell our great father, the President, the words his children speak.

"We made a treaty at Payne's Landing to go to the west; we were told to send some of our principal chiefs to examine the country, and if they approved of it, that the treaty should be complete; they went and found the country good. Whilst there, they had a talk with General Stokes and the commissioners; they were told that the Seminoles and Creeks were of the same family; were to be considered as the same nation; and placed under the direction of the same agent. They answered, that the Seminoles were a large nation, and should have their own agent as before; that if our father, the President, would give us our own agent, our own blacksmith, and our ploughs, we would go to this country; *but of [if] he did not, we should be unwilling to remove;* that we should be amongst strangers; they might be friendly or they might be hostile to us, and we wanted our own agent whom we knew, who would be our friend, who would take care of us, would do us justice, and see justice done us by others.

"The commissioners replied, that our wishes were reasonable, and that they would do all they could to induce our great father to grant them. Our lands at the west are separated from those of the Creeks by the Canadian, a great river; and we think the Creeks should have their agent on one side, and we ours on the other.

"We have been unfortunate in the agents our father has sent us. Gen. Thompson, our present agent, is the friend of the Seminoles; we thought at first that he would be like the others, but we know better now; he has but one talk, and what he tells us is the truth; we want him to go with us; he told us he could not go, but he at last agreed to do so, if our great father will permit him; we know our father loves his red children, and will not let them suffer for want of a good agent. This is our talk, which we want you to send to our father, the President, hoping that we may receive an early answer."

The council then adjourned. Those to whom this speech was addressed, deemed it incumbent on them to disclose their opinions upon a subject which appeared to be in the Indian's estimation so vastly important, and they accordingly annexed the following, signed by nine of the officers:—"The undersigned beg leave to be excused for expressing their opinion on the foregoing proceedings. The subject of a separate agency has been an engrossing and all-important one with the Seminoles; they attach to it a consideration which, perhaps, it does not merit; but we are persuaded that its concession to them will be attended with the happiest results: it will confirm those who are already friendly, and be the means of conciliating others who are hostile, or at least neutral. Under this view of the case, we cheerfully unite with the foregoing chiefs, that General Wiley Thompson be appointed their resident agent.

"In justice to General Thompson, we feel called upon to say, that he has done every thing in his power to dissuade the Indians from the course they have pursued in this matter; he assured them that they would have at the west an agent who would do them justice and protect them in their rights; and further, that it was an appointment he did not solicit, but could not reject if, by accepting it, he could advance their interests and facilitate their future operations."

This document was forwarded to the Secretary of War by General Clinch, with the following pertinent remarks:—"In forwarding to you the enclosed document, I beg leave to make a few remarks, although the subject to which it relates is, itself, of no great importance, yet it may have an important bearing on the present quiet and future happiness of these children of the forest. They are, from peculiar circumstances and long habit, suspicious of the white man. It is hard to induce them to believe that all the efforts and operations of the government are intended for their own good. The question of a separate agency was again and again brought forward by the chiefs last winter and spring, and appeared to be considered by them of the first importance to their future interest, prosperity and happiness; and it was at the earnest and repeated solicitations of the chiefs, that Lieutenant Harris and myself consented to incorporate their wishes on that subject, in the arrangement made with them in April last. Great pains have been taken to convince them, that the agent for the Creeks west of the Mississippi would watch over and protect them and their interests, in common with that of the Creeks, but I fear without effect. It is a law of nature for the weak to be suspicious of the strong. They say that the Creeks are much more numerous and powerful than they are; that there is a question of property, involving the right to a great many negroes, to be settled between them and the Creeks; and they are afraid that justice will not be done them, unless they can have a separate agent to watch over and protect their interests. The manly and straight forward course pursued towards them by Gen. Thompson, appears to have gained him their confidence, and they have again petitioned the President to make him their agent, and have requested me, through the immediate commanding officer at Fort King, to forward their petition with such remarks as my long acquaintance with their views and interest would authorize me to make. The experiment they are about to make is one of deep interest to them. They are leaving the birth place of their wives and children, and many of them the graves of those they held most dear; and is it not natural that they should feel, and feel deeply, on such a trying occasion, and wish to have some one that they had previously known, whom they could lean on, and look up to for protection?"

This earnest and pathetic appeal to the government was answered, as have been all their supplications, by a cold and stern negative, or they have been informed that their great father, the President, has been "made very angry" by their audacity in pleading for their just rights. The Indians, therefore, being naturally suspicious of the white man's intention towards them, have accordingly prepared themselves to resist a forcible removal.

The Long Swamp and Big Swamp Indians (principally the Micosukee tribe) were, from the causes heretofore stated,[*] again reduced to the greatest distress for the want of provisions, and their depredations upon the neighbouring settlements became daily more extensive. On one of these occasions three of the Long Swamp Indians were surprised, and two of them secured by the owner of the land, who tied them by the hands and feet with a rope, and carried them to his barn, where they were confined, without sustenance, for three days, unable to extricate themselves, and obliged to remain in one position. Not returning to their homes, their friends became alarmed for their safety, and the chief of the town where they resided went forward and demanded them. Being refused, he returned to his town, and, taking several of his people with him, he again demanded the release of the prisoners, and was again refused, with a threat by the white fellows that if the chief dared to effect their release, complaint should be entered against him. Upon this the whole party rushed to the barn, whence they heard the moaning of their friends, and there they beheld a most pitiable sight. The rope with which these poor fellows were tied had worn through into the flesh—they had temporarily lost the use of their limbs, being unable to stand or walk—they had bled profusely, and had received no food during their confinement—so, it may readily be imagined that they presented a horrible picture of suffering. The owner of the barn in which they were confined, then fired upon the Indians and slightly wounded one of the party, when their exasperation attained to such a height that, in retaliation for this

---

[*] Namely, the severe drought of the preceding season, and their being daily liable to be called on to remove.

brutal outrage, they set fire to the barn, and would not permit the owner to remove anything therefrom, nor did they leave the spot until the whole was consumed.

These outrages continued to increase with each succeeding week, and the Indians, discovering the hopelessness of their situation, at once concluded to oppose the efforts of the government, and call for a general assemblage of the nation. This course was rendered the more imperative at this particular period, in consequence of a demand having been made upon the Seminoles for a surrender of their cattle, ponies, hogs, &c., which were to be collected at some convenient depot, appraised and sold by the agent, and the Indians reimbursed therefor [*sic*], on their arrival in their new country. Those who were friendly to emigration, acquiesced in the views of the agent, and at once delivered over their stock and made preparations for leaving the country. Six of the principal chiefs, viz., Charley Amathla, Holata Amathla, Fucta Lusta Hajo, Otulkee Amathla, Conhatkee Mico and Foshutchee Mico having returned their cattle, ponies, and hogs, the agent then publicly announced that a sale of the same would take place on the first of the ensuing month, (December, 1835;) but in consequence of the interference of the anti-removal party the delivery of others was prevented, and the sale was necessarily postponed to an indefinite period. In the mean time the great meeting of the nation at Big Swamp resolved upon retaining possession of their country, and condemned all, who should oppose their views, to instant death. This, therefore, was the signal for an immediate abandonment of the friendly towns, and no time was lost by those who had gone too far to retract, in seeking the protection of the forts. Accordingly, Holata Amathla, Otulkee Amathla, Fucta Lusta Hajo, Conhatkee Mico and Foshutchee Mico, with about four hundred and fifty of their people, fled to Fort Brooke on the 9th of November, and encamped on the opposite side of the Hillsboro' river. (*See map for the camp of friendly Indians.*)

COMMENCEMENT OF HOSTILITIES.

THE chiefs of the anti-removal party becoming alarmed at the retreat of Holata Amathla and his people, and fearing that the proceedings of their secret council had been divulged, forthwith commenced securing all who remained in the upper towns, and forced them to raise their arms in assertion of their rights. On the 26th of November, a party of about four hundred warriors, headed by Holata Mico, Abraham and Assiola, proceeded to the residence of Charley Amathla, who was preparing also to retreat, and demanded a pledge from him that he and his people would oppose the intended project of forcible removal. But that Indian nobly replied, that he had already pledged his word that he would abide by the promise which he made to their great father, and that if his life paid the forfeit he felt bound to adhere to that promise. He said that he had lived to see his nation a ruined and degraded people, and he believed that their only salvation was, in removing to the west; he had made arrangements for his people to go, and had delivered to the agent all their cattle, so that they had no excuse now for not complying with their engagements. One of the chiefs then informed him that the crisis was come: he must either join them in their opposition, or suffer death, and that two hours would be allowed him to consult his people and give his determination. He replied, that his mind was unalterable, and his people could not make him break his word; that if he must die he hoped they would grant him time enough to make some arrangements for the good of his people. At this moment Assiola raised his rifle and was about to fire, when Abraham arrested the murderous aim, and requested them all to retire for a council with the other chiefs. Assiola, with a small party, however, separated themselves from the main body of the Indiaus [*sic*], and returned to Charley Amathla's, and shot him. Thirteen of Amathla's people immediately escaped to Fort King, while the others, deterred by their fears, remained until the return of the principal band, when they joined the hostile party. A more noble, intelligent, honest chief than Amathla, was not to be found in the Seminole nation, and he died by the hands of the very man, who, but a few months before, was released from confinement at the solicitation of his victim, and by his becoming security for his (Assiola's) good conduct!

This was the signal for a general outbreak of their vengeance, and they immediately abandoned their towns and assembled at Long Swamp to deliberate upon the future security of their families. In two days after, they retreated from this swamp, carefully concealing their trail, so that their present abode has been a subject of various and multiplied conjecture and astonishment. It is most probable, however, that the "cove," as it is termed, or the immense swamp and chain of lakes which surround and envelope a part of the Ouithlacoochee river, now shelters them from a possibility of discovery by our troops. The latter, under General Clinch, in April, penetrated into it several miles, but were unable to discover any traces of a settlement, although two Indian women, who were carried off from Fort Drane by the hostiles and subsequently made their escape, allege that our army passed within three miles of their present location.

Marauding parties now commenced their operations, almost simultaneously, in various sections of the adjoining country, pillaging and destroying every thing of value. Those who had inflicted injuries on the Indians were forthwith repaid, and many barely escaped with their lives. Conflagration succeeded conflagration until the whole country from Fort Brooke to Fort King was laid waste; while those who lived in the interior were compelled to abandon their crops, their stock, their implements of husbandry, furniture, and indeed every article of value, and seek protection within the Forts, or concentrate themselves in the neighbouring towns, around which pickets[*] were erected for their better security.

The whole military force now stationed in Florida, amounted to four hundred and eighty-nine men, including officers, and were distributed as follows: At St. Augustine, one company, fifty three men, including officers; at Fort Brooke on Hillsboro' Bay, three companies, one hundred and thirty-thee [sic] men; at Fort King, six companies, three hundred and three men.

When the news of the death of Charley Amathla reached Fort King, General Clinch immediately decided upon attacking a body of Micosukees who had assembled in the neigh-

---

[*] The pickets are made by splitting pine logs about eighteen feet in length into two parts, and driving them upright and firmly into the ground close together, with the flat side inwards; these are braced together by a strip of board nailed on the inside. The tops are sharpened, and holes are cut seven or eight feet from the ground for the fire arms. A range of benches extends around the work about three feet high, from which the fire is delivered. All our forts in that country are so formed.

bourhood of the forks of the Ouithlacoochee river, and should
he succeed in routing them it would drive terror among the
timid and wavering, and perhaps effectually silence the efforts
of others in creating disaffection among them. In pursuance of
his plans, he issued orders to the commanding officer at Fort
Brooke to put two companies in motion on the 16th of December, so as to form a junction with the troops from Fort
King, at or near the forks of the Ouithlacoochee. This order
was however suspended by Major. F. S. Belton,[47] the commanding officer at that station, in consequence of his very limited force (having but one hundred and twenty men) to protect
the garrison, and from information which he had previously
received of the strong position which the Indians occupied on
that river, and of which Gen. Clinch was promptly advised.
This plan was therefore deferred till the arrival of other forces.

In the mean time Generals Call and Hernandez[48] urged the
employment of a mounted militia force for the protection of
the frontier; to which solicitations, on the 9th of December,
the Department yielded, and, at the same time, apprised General Hernandez, that, at *his* request, orders would be given
through the Ordnance Department to issue five hundred muskets and the necessary equipments to the militia. But the ordnance master found it difficult to comply with a requisition for
a fourth of that number of muskets, and as for military stores,
he was quite destitute; he had no cartridges on hand, and the
powder was returned unfit for use. The militia were therefore
obliged to furnish themselves with horses, arms, ammunition,
provisions, &c., for thirty days, the period for which they volunteered, presuming that the difficulties would by that time be
overcome.

On the 7th of December a party of fourteen mounted men proceeded on a scout towards Wacahouta, the plantation of Captain Gabriel Priest, and when within one mile of the place they came upon a small hammock, through which some of the party declined passing. Four of them, however, dashed into it, and before they reached the middle, a party of Indians arose from ambush and fired on the two that were in the advance, and wounded them both. A Mr. Foulke received a bullet in his neck which passed down through his shoulder, but he was quickly picked up by those in the rear and borne off. The other was a son of Captain Priest; he had his arm broken, and his horse was shot dead under him; he fled, and sunk his body in a swamp until the Indians disappeared, when he returned to Miconopy.

About the same time a party of Indians attacked a number of men who were employed by the government to cut live oak on Drayton's Island, at the lower part of Lake George, but the men happily escaped the vengeance of the enemy by taking to their boats; two only were wounded.

On the 18th of December Colonel Warren,[49] of the militia, put his command in motion to scour a large hammock, near Wacahouta, where he supposed the Indians were imbodied [sic]; and not wishing to be encumbered with baggage, he directed Doctor (afterwards Major) M'Lemore,[50] with an escort of thirty men, to proceed direct with the train to Witumky, whither he would march on his return. When the train reached the Kenapaha (Payne's) prairie, fifty or sixty Indians arose from ambush and opened a very spirited fire upon the guard, killing eight and wounding six; the others retired to Miconopy.

The Indians also killed five of the horses, and wounded six more; they then took possession of the baggage, ammunition, &c., and set the wagon on fire.

On the 20th, Colonels Parish[51] and Read,[52] at the head of about one hundred men from Leon and Gadsden counties, took up a line of march for the purpose of reconnoitering the battle ground of the 18th, and gathering the remains of the baggage, &c. When near the place, they discovered the house of a Mr. Hogan on fire, and the Indians about leaving it. On the arrival of the advance guard at the house, a party of twenty-seven of the Seminoles kept them amused until the main body came up, when they retreated to a small hammock, which was quickly surrounded by the troops, leaving them no chance of escape. Both of the brave Colonels rushed into the hammock at the head of a detachment, and, in less than fifteen minutes, killed all but four of the enemy. The whites had four very severely wounded in this engagement.

Three of the hostile party came into the camp of the friendly Indians, near Fort Brooke, on the evening of the 22nd December, for the purpose, they said, of delivering a talk from Miconopy, of a pacific or neutral character. Whilst engaged in full council with Holata Amathla and the other chiefs and warriors, Major Belton was informed of the circumstance, and he ordered them to be detained and carried to the fort. When they found themselves ensnared, they no longer concealed their true character. Finding it necessary to communicate with General Clinch, then at Fort King, Major Belton sent the youngest and best runner with a letter, which, being upon the subject of the premeditated attack of the 31st December, involved many details. To guard against treachery, as the road passed through Abraham's lands, Major Belton stated numbers and other material facts in *French*. Two days beyond the time allowed, the messenger returned to Fort Brooke, bringing a talk from Hitchiti Mico and Abraham, stating that his (Major Belton's) talk was good, and that he might expect them on the 30th. It was then evident that the Indians had intercepted the letter, and were well aware of the intended attack.

Major Dade was present at the council of the warriors on that evening, and the proceedings being interpreted to him, he expressed every confidence in Indian character, and his conviction of the sincerity which governed the friendly chiefs; he also believed that Abraham, a domestic of Miconopy, had great influence over his chief.

The expected reinforcement of thirty-nine men from Key West, with the gallant brevet Major Dade, having arrived on the 21st, no time was lost in preparing the two companies, ordered by General Clinch on the 16th, to form a junction with the forces at Fort King. Accordingly, at six o'clock, A. M., of the 24th, Captain Gardiner's[53] company C, 2nd artillery, and Captain Fraser's[54] company B, 3d infantry [ed: Potter is in error, it was the 3rd Artillery], making fifty bayonets each, with eight officers, taking with them ten days' provisions, one six pounder drawn by four oxen, and one light one-horse wagon, were placed in the line of march for that post, under command of Captain Gardiner.

In the chain of events, it may not be amiss to notice the change which occurred in the command of this ill-fated detachment, since it shows the noble and generous impulses of his heart and is so perfectly characteristic of Major Dade.

From his company A, 4th infantry, amounting to thirty-nine men, the two companies of Captain Fraser and Gardiner were made up. Captain Gardiner's lady was exceedingly ill, and it was much feared that if he then left her she would die. He however made every preparation for a start, and was present at *reveillie* [*sic*] on the morning of the 24th, and mounted his horse in front of the detachment. At this juncture Major Dade voluntarily proposed to Major Belton, the commanding officer at the post, that he (Dade) should take Captain Gardiner's place. The proposition was immediately accepted, and the command moved on. Before they had proceeded far, Captain Gardiner ascertained that the transport schooner Motto was on the eve of leaving for Key West, where Mrs. Gardiner's father and children were; he concluded to place Mrs. Gardiner on board the vessel, and gratify his wishes by going with his company. He soon after joined it, but the peculiar relation in which he now stood to Major Dade induced him to let the latter continue in command.

The oxen which drew the field piece having broken down when only four miles from Fort Brooke, the command proceeded to a branch of the Hillsborough river, six miles from the fort, and there encamped for the night; from that place Major Dade sent an express to Major Belton, and requested him to forward the field piece as soon as possible. Horses were therefore immediately purchased, and the piece reached the column that night about nine o'clock. Taking up the line of march on the morning of the 25th, they reached the Hillsborough river, but found the bridge had been burnt and destroyed, and they encamped there until the morning. The difficulty of crossing here retarded their movements very much, and on the 26th, they made but six miles.—On the 27th, they crossed the Big and Little Ouithlacoochee rivers, and encamped about three miles north of the latter branch. Up to this time Major Dade being aware that the enemy was continually watching his movements, had adopted every precaution against surprise or attack at night, by throwing up a small breastwork. Early on the morning of the 28th, the ill-fated party were again in motion, and when about four miles from their last camp, the advanced guard passed a plat of high grass, and having reached a thick cluster of palmettos, about fifty yards beyond the grass, (*see map of the massacre,*) a very heavy and destructive fire was opened upon them by the unseen enemy, at a distance of fifty or sixty yards, which literally mowed them down, and threw the main column into the greatest confusion. Soon recovering, however, on observing the enemy rise in front of them, they made a charge, and plied their fire so unerringly, that the Indians gave way, but not until muskets were clubbed, knives and bayonets used, and the combatants were clinched; they were finally driven off to a considerable distance. Major Dade having fallen dead on the first fire, the command devolved upon Captain Gardiner, and as he discovered the Indians gathering again about a half mile off, he directed a breastwork to be thrown up for their protection, but the enemy allowed them so little time that it was necessarily very low (only two and a half feet high) and imperfect. The Indians being reinforced, and having stationed about a hundred of their mounted warriors on the opposite side to cut off retreat, they slowly and cautiously advanced to a second attack, yelling and whooping in so terrific a manner as to drown the reports of the fire-arms. The troops soon began to make their great gun speak, which at first kept the enemy at bay, but soon surrounding the little breastwork they shot down every man who attempted to work the gun, so that it was rendered almost useless to them. One by one these brave and heroic men fell by each other's side in the gallant execution of their duty to their country. Being obliged by the ineffective field work to lay down to load and fire, the poor fellows laboured under great disadvantages, as in the haste with which the work was constructed they selected the lowest spot about that part, and consequently gave the enemy doubly the advantage over them. Major Dade and his horse, Captain Fraser, with nearly every man of the advance guard, fell dead on the first volley, besides a number of the main column. Lieutenant Mudge[55] received a mortal wound the first fire, and, on gaining the breastwork, breathed his last. Lieutenant Keayes [Keais][56] had both arms broken, also on the first attack; and one of the men bound them up with a handkerchief and placed him against a tree near the breastwork, where he was soon after tomahawked by a negro. Lieutenant Henderson[57] received a severe wound in the left arm, but he heroically struck to the fight and fired thirty or forty shots before he died. Dr. Gatlin[58] posted himself behind a log in the centre of the work, and exclaimed that he had four barrels for them; but, poor fellow, he soon ceased to use them, as he was shot early in the second attack. Towards the close of the battle poor Gardiner received his death shot in the breast, outside of the enclosure, and fell close to Lieutenant Mudge; the command of the little party then fell on Lieutenant Bassinger [Basinger],[59] who observed, on seeing Captain Gardiner fall, "I am the only officer left, boys; we must do the best we can." He continued at his post about an hour after Gardiner's death, when he received a shot in the thigh which brought him down. Shortly after this their ammunition gave out, and the Indians broke into the enclosure, and every man was either killed, or so badly wounded as to be unable to make resistence [*sic*], took off their fire arms and whatever else would be of service to them and retreated. Sometime after the Indians left, the negroes came inside of the breastwork and began to mutilate the bodies of those who showed the least signs of life, when Bassinger sprang upon his feet and implored them to spare him; they heeded not his supplications, but struck him down with their hatchets, cut open his breast and tore out his heart and lungs; such is the report of Clarke[60] [Clark], the only survivor. However, I must confess that the appearance of the body on the 20th of February did not seem to indicate that such violence had been committed on *him*, although one of the slain (a private) was found in a truly revolting condition—a part of his body had been cut off and crammed into his mouth! The negroes stripped all the officers and some of the men of their clothing, but left many valuables upon their persons, which were discovered upon examination by Major Mountfort,[61] of General Gaines'[62] command, and an account carefully taken by the Major, in order to transfer the articles respectively to the deceased's relatives. All the military stores were carried off except the field piece, which they spiked and conveyed to the pond, as marked on the map of the battle ground.

Private John Thomas[63] [ed.: the account of survivors is in error; see endnote] arrived at Fort Brooke the following day, having been wounded in the thigh and made his escape in the early part of the action. On the 31st, Private Ransom Clark, the only present survivor, returned to Fort Brooke with five severe wounds: one in the right shoulder, one in the right thigh, one near the right temple, one in the arm, and another in his back. This is the second miraculous escape which this individual has made. He was the only survivor of a whole boat's crew who, with Lieut. Chandler[64] of Fort Morgan, was drowned in Mobile Bay by the capsizing of a boat in January 1835. He is now pensioned by the government with the pitiful sum of *eight dollars per month!* Another private, by the name of Sprague,[65] followed the day after Clarke, and brought a cleft stick which he found stuck in a creek, to which was fastened a note from Capt. Fraser to Major Mountfort. As if dreading a lamentable end, he stated that they were beset by the enemy every night, and were pushing on.

The sufferings of Clarke and Sprague, particularly of the former, must have been most excruciating. Clarke says he crept on his hands and knees more than two thirds of the way, having travelled the sixty-five miles in about the same number of hours.

The force of the Indians could not have been less than three hundred and fifty men. This I judge of from the extent of ground which they must have covered while in ambush. Thomas estimated them at four hundred; Clarke's estimates vary from six hundred to one thousand; and Sprague thinks there were from five to eight hundred.

The officers who fell in this battle were—

Brevet Major F. L. Dade, of the 4th Infantry,		-	1
Captain G. W. Gardiner,	2d Artillery,	-	1
" U. Fraser, -	3d do.	-	1
Lieut. W. E. Bassinger,	2d do.	-	1
" R. Henderson,	2d do.	-	1
" Mudge -	3d do.	-	1
" J. L. Keayes,-	3d do.	-	1
Ass't Surg. Gatlin, U. S. A.,		- -	1

Officers,	8
Non-commissioned officers and privates,	96
Interpreter *Louis* and a servant,[66]	2
Buried by the army of Gen. Gaines	106
Killed, day after the battle,	1
Escaped, of which only one remains,	3
	110

The attack was made at about 10 o'clock, A. M., and continued with little or no intermission, save that after the first repulsion, until between three and four o'clock, P. M. The chosen ground of the Indians seemed to be very injudicious, being an open pine woods with very little undergrowth, and excepting the grass and clustered palmettos, on the right of the road, (*see map,*) afforded them no shelter. But they well knew of the small force against which they were to contend, and their object in selecting that ground was to massacre the whole party, and not leave one to tell the sad tale of their destruction; whereas if they had attacked in a thick and dense country many more would have escaped. Wahoo Swamp, the residence of Jumper and his people, was four miles west, and Pilaklakaha, the home of Miconopy, was four miles east from the massacre ground; but these towns were deserted immediately succeeding the murder of Charley Amathla.

In the course of events I shall necessarily refer once more to the massacre ground of poor Dade and his companions in arms, and will attempt to describe the scene which we witnessed on the 20th of February, seven weeks after the enactment of the horrible tragedy.

Whilst this unequal battle was raging forty miles south of Fort King, the death of General Thompson and others was effected within a few hundred yards of that post. This occurred on the afternoon of the 28th, between three and four o'clock. "The troops, with the exception of Captain Lendrum's[67] company of the third artillery, about *forty* strong, had been withdrawn on the 26th, to reinforce General Clinch at Lang Syne plantation, preparatory to his striking a blow at the families of the Indians, supposed to be concealed in the swamps and hammocks of the Ouithlacoochee river, with the hope of bringing on a general engagement. The departure of the detachment had rendered precaution more necessary, and all those attached to the fort or agency had been required to move within the picketing. General Thompson slept within the defences, and passed a greater part of the day at the agency office, about a hundred yards beyond the works. The sutler (Mr. [Erastus] Rogers) had moved his goods into the fort, but was in the habit of eating his meals at his house, about six hundred yards off, skirting a thick hammock to the south-west of the fort.

On the day of the massacre, Lieut. [Constantine] Smith, of the 2d artillery, had dined with the General, and after dinner invited him to take a stroll with him. They had not proceeded more than three hundred yards beyond the agency office when they were fired upon by a party of Indians, who rose from ambush in the hammock, within sight of the fort, and on which the *sutler's* house borders. The reports of the first rifles fired, the war-whoop twice repeated, and, after a brief space, several other volleys more remote and in the quarter of Mr. Rogers' house, were heard, and the smoke of the firing seen at the fort.

Upon the first alarm Capt. Lendrum drew in his men, who were for the most part busily engaged without the pickets, securing and strengthening the defences. Expecting an assault from the hammock immediately fronting and flanking the fort, and not then knowing of the absence of General Thompson and the others, he supposed the firing was but a feint to draw him out to be cut off. Shortly after, however, the fact was made known to him, and about the same time several whites and coloured people, who had escaped from the sutler's house, came running in and apprised Capt. Lendrum that Mr. Rogers, his clerks and themselves had been surprised at dinner, and that the three former had fallen into the hands of the Indians. A command was instantly despatched [*sic*] to succour and pursue, if not too late. But the butchery had been as brief as it was complete, and the last whoop that had been heard was the signal for a precipitate retreat, and the savage perpetrators were already beyond the reach of our small force."

The bodies of Gen. Thompson, Lieut. Smith and Mr. Kitzler, were soon found and brought in; those of the others were only found on the following morning. That of Gen. Thompson was perforated with *fourteen* bullets, and a deep knife wound in the right breast. Those of Lieut. Smith and Mr. Kitzler had each received two bullets, and the head of the latter was so broken that the brains had come out. The bodies of Mr. Rogers and Robert Suggs were most shockingly mangled; the heads of each very much broken; the body of Mr. Rogers was penetrated by *seventeen* bullets, and that of Suggs by two. All, saving the latter, were *scalped.*

An old black woman, the cook of Mr. Rogers, concealed herself behind some barrels under the counter of a back room which had formerly been the store, and she stated that *Assiola* came into the room, battering down the furniture and whatever else chanced to be in his way, and expressed great disappointment on discovering that Mr. Rogers had removed his goods. In a few moments after she heard him give a shrill yell, when the whole body of the Indians immediately retreated. It was the opinion of those who escaped, that the party consisted of fifty or sixty Micosukees, under command of Assiola, and two other chiefs whom they did not know, but whose attire denoted them to be leaders.—The peculiar and shrill war yell of Assiola was distinctly heard and recognized by two or three friendly Indians at Fort King.

Two expresses were despatched upon fresh horses on the evening of this horrid tragedy, with tidings of it to General Clinch; they took different directions, and one of them made a narrow escape, though both arrived in safety.

General Call with Colonels Parish and Leigh Read having arrived on the 29th, at the head of nearly five hundred brave volunteers from the adjoining counties, who had previously been ordered to scour the country on the right and left flank, and formed a junction with the United States troops, amounting to about two hundred effective men, under the gallant and noble Clinch. This officer issued orders for the troops to move at sunrise on the 29th December. They arrived within half a mile of the Ouithlacoochee on the 30th, and encamped for the night, carefully adopting every measure against surprise and to secure concealment. A breastwork was thrown up to afford them protection in case of attack at night, and no fires were allowed in the camp after dark. At daybreak the following morning the column again resumed its march towards the river, leaving the baggage train in charge of a small detachment under Lieut. Dancy,[68] U. S. A., at the camp. On arriving at the crossing place the General found that his guides had deceived him, and that the river was not fordable, but deep, and the current very rapid. No Indians having been seen along the banks, one of the men swam over and obtained a small canoe from the opposite side, in which the regulars commenced to cross, but as seven men only could pass at a time, it was excessively tedious work. General Clinch and Colonels [Samuel] Parkhill and Read having passed to the other side of the river, they, in conjunction with Gen. Call on this side, immediately commenced to construct a raft of logs, so as to accelerate the movements of the troops, and to pass their baggage, &c. The regulars having all crossed by twelve o'clock, Major Fanning[69] marched them by a sinuous trail, which led into an open field surrounded on all sides by a thick swamp and hammock, and formed them into line, waiting for the crossing of the volunteers. When about fifty of the latter had reached the opposite shore, and while the officers were superintending the construction of the raft, they were suddenly surprised with the cry, of "the Indians are coming." Every man flew to his post, and the moment General Call drew up his men in line, the Indians opened a fire upon them from the opposite side, but the volunteers poured a heavy volley into the hammock, which silenced the enemy; who now finding that some of our troops had crossed, collected their force and opened a desperate and destructive fire on the regulars. General Clinch discovering that the enemy had the advantage of the ground, ordered a "charge," which was most gallantly executed by Major Fanning, but the Indians still maintained their ground. "Charge again!" and then another drove them some distance off. The chiefs called to their warriors to rally once more and not to run from the "pale faces"—that the Ouithlacoochee divided their enemies from them—that the regulars were a mere handful, and could be soon overcome;—but all their efforts were in vain; they had been whipped severely enough by the gallant little handful, and were well satisfied that there was no contending against the firmness of American soldiery. The battle was a very severe and hotly contested one, and lasted for seventy minutes, during which we sustained a heavy loss, but probably not so great as that of the enemy, who were seen incessantly carrying off their dead and wounded during the engagement.

During the battle General Call, Colonel Warren and Major Cooper,[70] with a number of volunteers, crossed the river at imminent hazard, and the two latter officers immediately engaged and fought with the most determined bravery. General

Call formed the volunteers that last crossed into two parallel lines, posting one above and one below the crossing place, for the purpose of protecting the troops on the other side, and those who were recrossing with the dead and wounded upon the temporary bridge of logs; he was therefore unable to reach the field until after the enemy were silenced, although his services were eminently useful in directing the crossing; too much praise cannot be awarded him. From the peculiar disposition of the Indian forces, nothing short of the brave and determined spirit which our troops manifested, in charging into the hammocks and routing the enemy from their fastnesses, could possibly have saved them from sharing the fate of poor Dade. During the battle a large number of Indians were observed to come up and join the others, and after the firing ceased a soldier's knapsack was found upon the field, which created much uneasiness as to the fate of the detachment which had been expected from Fort Brooke, (Maj. Dade's;) and it was not until sometime in February that General Clinch was advised of the disaster which had befallen it. The troops retained the field for about three hours after the enemy disappeared—until the wounded and dead had been recrossed, and the horses swam over. They then returned to the opposite side to bury their dead, and encamped within the enclosure of the preceding night.

The time of service of the volunteers having expired the same day on which the battle took place, and they being anxious to return to the protection of their families, Gen. Clinch took up a line of march, and arrived on the 2nd January at Fort Drane, where he disbanded them.

The officers engaged in this battle did honour to themselves; the names of CLINCH, GRAHAM, FANNING, WARREN, CALL, COOPER, READ have shed a lustre upon the military character of our country which must ever be dearly remembered. Here let it be recorded, that two hundred and twenty-seven of "the pale faces" gallantly sustained themselves, and, in one hour, drove more than seven hundred yelling savages, of the most determined and ferocious spirit, from their own fastnesses, and chastized [sic] them with the utmost severity! The cool and intrepid conduct of the noble Clinch was extraordinarily displayed; he was present during the whole period, in the hottest of the fight, and had his cap perforated by a ball which grazed his hair; another passing through the sleeve of his coat, he coolly remarked, "*I do believe those fellows are firing at me.*" Major Fanning also distinguished himself; and Captain William M. Graham,[71] of the fourth infantry, deserves the highest praise for his gallant and heroic conduct, having received no less than three wounds while leading his company to the charge; a braver or more excellent officer cannot be found. Lieutenant Campbell Graham[72] and Lieut. Ridgely[73] also evinced much bravery. The volunteer officers, to whom should be apportioned a good share of the glory in routing the enemy, are, the brave and gallant Major (now Brigadier General) Leigh Read, whose horse was shot under him; Col. John Warren; Col. Parkhill (of Richmond, Va.;) Col. Mills;[74] Major Cooper, Captain [James] Scott, (of Richmond, Va.,) and Capt. [William] Bailey. Gen. Call's services, although not brought into action in the field, were most eminently displayed— indeed his absence would have been sincerely felt. Majors Gamble[75] and Wellford were also highly spoken of. General Clinch also pays a well merited compliment to Major J. S.

Lytle,[76] (his aid [*sic*],) Captains Drane, Mellon[77] and Gates;[78] Lieutenants Talcott,[79] Capron,[80] John Graham,[81] Maitland[82] and Brooks[83] of the United States' army; and Col. M'Intosh, Lieutenants Youman,[84] Stewart, Hunter and [John] Cuthbert, and Adjutant Phillips, of the Florida volunteers. Of the officers of the medical staff, Drs. Weightman,[85] Hamilton, [James] Randolph and Brandon, he expresses a high opinion.

The returns of the killed and wounded in this battle, are as follows:

REGULARS.

Killed,	2 artificers and 2 privates,		4
Wounded,	1 Captain and 2 Lieuts.	3	
	2 Serj'ts and 4 Corporals,	6	
	Privates,	<u>43</u>	52

VOLUNTEERS.

Wounded,	Col. Warren, Major Cooper, and Lieut. Youman,	3		
	Privates,	4	7	<u>59</u>
Aggregate killed and wounded,				<u>63</u>

Previous to, and immediately succeeding this battle, the Indians spread themselves in small parties for the purpose of devastating the country. They appeared simultaneously in the south part of the peninsula, as far north as Picolata, and from the extreme east below St. Augustine to the west, carrying off every thing that was useful to them and destroying the remainder. At New river, on the south-east side of the peninsula, they murdered the wife, children and teacher in the family of Mr. Cooley, on the 5th of January, in whose house they knew that a parcel of goods were stored. They carried off twelve barrels of provisions, thirty hogs, three horses, one keg of powder, over two hundred pounds of lead, seven hundred dollars worth of dry goods, four hundred and eighty dollars in silver, and two negroes. Mr. Cooley was absent at the time. Who can even imagine the distress of the once happy, now bereaved husband and father, who, on returning to those most dear to him, discovered their bodies lying savagely murdered at the threshold of his door! His wife he found shot through the heart and her infant child in her arms, and his two eldest children also shot in the same place: the girl still held her book in her hand, and the boy's lay at his side. His house was also burned. All the settlements in that neighbourhood, (two hundred and fifty miles south of St. Augustine,) were immediately abandoned, and the inhabitants flew to the Light house on Cape Florida for protection; but they had scarcely been settled here when the Indians made their appearance, and they were obliged to seek shelter elsewhere.

The scene of destruction on the east side of the peninsula, and along the St. Johns river, is truly heart-rending. At Spring Garden on the St. Johns, the extensive plantations of Colonel Rees, (who is the largest sufferer in the territory,) was entirely laid waste and his buildings burnt. Mr. A. Forrester's loss is immense. His splendid plantation, with cane sufficient to manufacture ninety hogsheads of sugar, was destroyed, besides thirty hogsheads of sugar ready for market, and one hundred and sixty-two negroes were carried off; a large number of mules and horses were also taken, and a Mr. Woodruff and a negro killed. In this neighborhood alone it is supposed that more than three hundred negroes have been carried away. Pursuing their outrages further down, they in course burnt the establishment of Doctor Brush, near Pilatka, Mr. Hatch's house and several others—extending their destruction to a distance of eighteen miles from Picolata, where they burnt the house of Mr. Solano.[86] But their principal ravages have been along the east side, from St. Augustine to the south, wherever a settlement could be found. Near the Halifax river they destroyed the buildings of Mr. Depeyster, with whose negroes they formed a league, and being supplied by them with a boat, crossed the river and fired the establishment of Mr. Dummett; but a faithful servant who had concealed himself when he found the Indians approaching, succeeded in extinguishing the flames before they attained much headway. Major Heriot's plantation was laid waste—his houses were consumed, and eighty of his negroes moved off with the Indians. At Dunlawton, the plantation of Mrs. Anderson, the rascals met with a warm reception by a small command of forty men, under the command of Major Putnam,[87] who had been ordered to take post at Bulow's,[88] but on hearing that the Indians were at the work of destruction near Dunlawton, he resolved to proceed there with despatch. On his arrival in the neighbourhood the houses on that plantation were found burning, and the Indians not being aware of their arrival, Major Putnam placed his men in the rear of the smouldering ruins in two negro houses, near to a pen in which was a large number of cattle, which he supposed the Indians intended to drive off the next morning. At daylight two Indians were observed to approach, when Captain Dummett gave the signal by firing at the foremost, and the whole command rushed out upon them. The

men were ordered to retreat nearer to the river in order to prevent their being cut off by a large body of the enemy who
were seen coming towards them, and as soon as they had
gained their positions near the river, a heavy fire was opened
upon them and the contest waxed very warm for about twenty
minutes, when the Major ordered a retreat to the boats, as he
discovered the enemy, already amounting to about one hundred and fifty were about to be reinforced. The descent from
the shore being very gradual, and the boats being at a considerable distance from the landing and aground, the enemy were
enabled to do them much injury, as many of them in retreating
had not taken the precaution to hold their guns up, the locks
got wet and were unfitted for use. The Indians attempted to
follow, but those who had dry guns were enabled to keep them
off. The command then returned to Bulow's. In this engagement the whites had three killed and fourteen wounded.

From this the enemy moved up towards St. Augustine, destroying the extensive plantations of General Hernandez,
whose loss is excessively great:—Mr. Samuel Williams' sugar
mills, dwelling and corn houses burned, and crop destroyed—
loss supposed to be nearly fifty thousand dollars. At Mr. Bulow's the destruction is enormous; the buildings alone are estimated at forty-eight thousand dollars. Then to Mr. Dupont's
at Buen Retiro, Mr. Dunham's, M'Rea's at Tomoka Creek,
Mr. Bayas', General Herring, Mr. Bartalone Solano's and
nearly every other plantation from St. Augustine, down, has
been laid waste, moveables carried off or destroyed, and the
buildings burned. The loss to these planters is incalculable—it
cannot fall far short of two millions of dollars in improvements alone, independent of the immense inconvenience

which they must suffer in not being able to make their crops.

A question naturally suggests itself here, which is bur-
thened [*sic*] with great interest to the whole community;—I
allude to the future indemnification of the owners for these
losses. Who must father them? The men who have done every thing within human power to avert the sad calamity—who
have constantly advised the government of the approach of the
dreadful evil, and flew like patriots to arms to protect their
properties from the ravages of the desolating foe—*or* should
that government, whose measures have produced the evil—
whose own neglect to profit by the humane and important
suggestions of the intelligent people of Florida—who, in consequence of not adopting these precautionary measures which
it was their sacred duty to regard—who might have placed a
sufficiently imposing military force in Florida to restrain the
Indians and effect the removal without detriment to the interests of its citizens, yet neglected so to do?

Who is to be mainly benefited by the removal of the Indians? Is it the planter, or the farmer whose lands are already
under cultivation, and who has as much as he can conveniently
manage; *or* is it the government, who, in exchanging lands
which could not be sold for at least a century, for the best and
most fertile region of Florida, will pocket five or six millions
of dollars by the operation? Can it for a moment be believed,
that the Congress of the United States will permit the citizens
of any portion of the country to be thrown from a state of independent affluence, into that of suffering penury, in their efforts to effect a favourite and humane measure of policy? No!
it cannot be, it would be an indelible stain upon the character

and honesty of our national councils.—While upon this subject it will perhaps be satisfactory to the reader to have the opinion of a distinguished jurist of our country, as to the justice of indemnification for these losses, and with that view it is given. It will be observed, that he has merely given authorities and touched the heads of arguments, but they may be instrumental in turning the attention of others to the subject.

"The reasons why the citizens of Florida, whose property has been destroyed by the Indians, should be reimbursed.

"The source from which they should be reimbursed, considered.

"Whether there be any difference between the situation of those, whose property was destroyed before the commencement of actual fighting, and that destroyed by the enemy afterwards?

"Whether there be any, and if any, what difference where the war was waged for causes just or unjust?

"The right of Postliminium is that in virtue of which, persons and things taken by the enemy, are restored to their former state, when coming again under the power of the nation to which they belonged.

" 'Naturally, (says Vattel)[89] goods of all kinds are recoverable by the rights of Postliminium, and could they be certainly known again, there is no intrinsic reason why moveables should be excepted.' Several instances of such a practice among the ancients are recited by Grotius,[90] book III. chap. xvi. section 2. The State is obligated to protect the goods and persons of its citizens, and defend them against the enemy: therefore, when a citizen or any part of his substance are fallen into the hands of the enemy, should any fortunate event bring them into the power of the State, it certainly is incumbent upon the State to restore them to their former owner, 'in a word, (says Vattel) *the State is bound to settle every thing as they were before they fell into the enemy's hands,*' and here the justice or injustice of the war makes no difference. If the war be just, they were unjustly taken, and thus nothing is more natural than to restore them as soon as it becomes possible. If the war be unjust, they are not bound to bear the calamities of it more than any other part of the nation. Hence, all the property taken by the enemy that is capable of being identified, is to be restored to the citizen. But it is necessary to consider another point arising here. If that property be rendered by such conquest of the enemy valueless, or of trifling comparative value to what it possessed before such capture and recapture, or be entirely destroyed by the committing of waste, such as burning dwellings, mills, barns, &c., is the difference in such value to be reimbursed, or such waste compensated by the State from its own treasury, or from the funds of the enemy? This necessarily involves the question of what the civilians term *expletio juris,* and on this point Vattel is very clear and unanswerable. He says: 'If it be lawful to carry off things belonging to an enemy, with a view of weakening him, and sometimes of punishing him, it is no less lawful in a just war to appropriate to ourselves those things as a compensation. They are detained as an equivalent for what is due by the enemy, for the expenses and *damages* which he has occasioned, and even when there is cause of punishing him, instead of the penalty which he has deserved. For when I cannot procure to myself the individual thing which belongs or is due to me, I have a right to an equivalent, which by the rules of *expletive justice,* and according to moral estimate, is considered as the thing itself. Thus war founded on justice is according to the law of nature, which constitutes the necessary law of nations, a just method of acquisition. And where a nation has to deal with a perfidious, restless and dangerous enemy, the State may greatly exceed exact repletive justice, and it may deprive such enemy of its towns and provinces, for it is allowable to weaken such an enemy. The lawful end of the penalty is future security. Such damages as are caused by inevitable necessity, such for instance as the destruction created by the havoc of artillery in retaking a town from the enemy, will not be remunerated by the State doing the damage to its citizens, because they are accidents and calamities arising from war. But the rule is otherwise as regards a perfidious enemy, who, void of all pretence, occasions the destruction of the houses of a town by artillery or otherwise. In such a case the State will reimburse the citizen from the funds of such enemy, whenever it is in its power to do so. And it is an universal principle, consentaneous to the duties of a nation, and consequently equitable, nay, just, to relieve as far as possible from its own funds, those who have been injured by the desolation of war."

Intelligence of the savage massacre of Major Dade and his heroic band, and the battle of General Clinch, with the subsequent conflagrations, having reached the adjoining states, immediate preparations were made to succour the troops in that quarter, and to save that fair portion of our country from further devastation by the ruthless foe. In pursuance of the authority vested in him, General Clinch made a requisition upon the governors of the states of Georgia, South Carolina and Alabama, for militia to aid the Floridians in their desperate struggle with the murderous gang; but, with a spirit which does honour to the American character, hundreds of the bravest sons of those states flew with eagerness to the standard and superseded the necessity of drafts being made. Meetings were organised in Augusta, Savannah, Darien and Charleston, at which the most enthusiastic feeling was evinced, and a few days after nearly two thousand volunteers were ready to embark at a moment's warning for the theatre of war.

At Charleston they exhibited the most elevated spirit. As the apathy displayed by the general Government, led to the belief that it would be some time before they would deign to listen to the calls of the sufferers, and "as great confusion seemed to prevail both in the War and Financial Departments, which threatened utter ruin to the poor inhabitants of Florida," they adopted resolutions to invite donations and the services of volunteers. As early as the first of January, a meeting was called and preparations were made to succour the distressed; but General Eustis[91] informed the officers, or committee appointed by the meeting that General Clinch had sufficient supplies and force under his command to subdue any number of Indians and negroes that could be opposed to him in Florida, which prevented supplies reaching them at an early day. Intelligence having been received from General Clinch on the 12th, with a requisition upon the Governor of South Carolina for six hundred men, the committee conferred with General Eustis, and requested him to send a company of the United States troops, with the requisite arms and ammunition, for the protection of St. Augustine. Accordingly they were put in readiness, and the committee chartered a steamboat and placed on board one thousand bushels of corn, one hundred barrels of flour, thirty barrels of beef, twenty barrels of pork, and ten tierces of rice, and started her to that place. This contribution of temporary aid to the citizens of St. Augustine was heartily responded to by them, but they earnestly invited a few volunteers to join them in protecting the city. Communications were also received from Jacksonville, on the St. Johns river, requesting such aid by the military and contributions of provisions as could be obtained.

About the 20th of January another meeting was called for the purpose of raising a body of volunteers, when several animating and spirit-stirring appeals were made to the Carolinians: But did they need it to excite in them an ardour for the cause of their 'common country'? No! the gallant sons of Carolina waited not for an *appeal* to *their* chivalry, but a thousand voices were raised in advocacy of the cause. The banks of Charleston immediately subscribed twenty-five thousand dollars as a loan to the government for the purchase of provisions and equipment of troops for Florida, and the gallant *Hamilton* addressed his brigade the following day in this manner: "The Brigadier General deems it altogether superfluous to make any appeal to the gallant men of his brigade, to meet with promptitude and spirit this call which has been made upon their patriotism in defence of an interesting portion of our common country; for he is deeply and proudly impressed with the gratifying conviction, that no state in this confederacy is better prepared than South Carolina, to discharge in the hour of peril, with alacrity and honour, its just obligations to the government of the union."

The committee also despatched a schooner loaded to the bends with corn, rice, bread, beef and pork, with considerable military and hospital stores, and a physician to attend on the sick and wounded at the posts at the St. Johns, and she arrived at Jacksonville midst the hearty gratulations of hundreds who had been driven from their homes by the savage foe, in the utmost destitution.

Four companies of volunteers, viz., the Washington Light Infantry, Captain [Henry] Ravenel; Washington Volunteers, Captain [J. E. B.] Finley; German Fusileers, Captain [W. H.] Timrod; and Hamburgh Volunteers, Captain [S. W.] Cunningham, were put in motion on the 27th of January, for St. Augustine. Having arrived there on the 30th, their services were immediately called into requisition, and details were made to scour the neighbourhood. On the 12th of February these volunteers were relieved from duty by the arrival of the South Carolina militia and the United States troops, under Major Kirby.[92] These fresh troops commenced scouring the country to the south, preparatory to concentrating themselves at Volusia, to constitute the "left wing;" but from the period of their arrival until about the 22d of March, they had no battle with the Indians.[*] An instance of the generous and chivalric spirit

---

[*] At daylight on the 10th of March, two men belonging to Captain Doucin's company, and one belonging to Captain Henry's, of Colonel Brisbane's regiment, were shot down while procuring wood. The two former were scalped, when the Indians retreated.

of Carolina, which occurred at a parade, is well worth recording. On the requisition of the Governor for three companies to be furnished for Florida, Colonel Chestnut of Camden called out his regiment. After making a speech to them, he asked those who desired to join in the cause of their suffering neighbours, to step forward. Upon the utterance of these words the *whole regiment* marched forward and tendered their services! It then became necessary to draft from them, for *all* were anxious to go, and would not submit to a selection. At the same time nearly four thousand dollars were subscribed for their equipment.

The reader's attention will now be drawn to the gallant spirits of Georgia. On the receipt of the distressing account of Major Dade's defeat, and the subsequent battle of General Clinch, (one company from Savannah having on the receipt of the earliest news of disturbances embarked for Picolata,) a meeting of the Richmond Blues and Richmond Hussars of Augusta, was convened for the purpose of volunteering their aid in protecting the ill-fated territory. The City Council, with a commendable liberality, appropriated such funds as were required to furnish arms, ammunition, &c., and every preparation was in progress to make an early start. The LADIES of Augusta *volunteered* to make up their uniforms, and in less than a week these gallant men of a gallant state were speeding their way to Picolata, on the St. Johns. These companies, as indeed most of the others, were composed of the very *elite* and wealthiest of the state. It had been intimated to Captain [Francis] Robertson and

Mr. Quartermaster Joseph Beard[*93] that Fort Drane and the posts on the St. Johns were poorly supplied with ordnance and Quartermaster's stores, and in consequence of this rumour, which was subsequently found to be too true, the Quartermaster purchased, with funds appropriated by the councils, and took from the arsenal one six pounder with the necessary equipments, three hundred rounds of grape, canister and round shot, ten thousand rounds of musket ball and buckshot cartridges, and a general supply of Quartermaster's stores. On the arrival of the company at Savannah, this officer increased his supplies by purchasing ten kegs of rifle powder, five hundred pounds of bar lead, and all the necessary articles for making rifle ball cartridges. Further supplies were drawn on their arrival at Picolata, amounting to five thousand rounds of musket ball and buckshot cartridges, two hundred rounds of grape and canister shot, and one six pounder with equipments. The foresight of Quartermaster Beard resulted most fortunately, as the military posts had, by the extreme and unpardonable negligence of the War Department, been reduced so bare, that, in case of attack, they must necessarily have fallen into the hands of the enemy. Nothing but the timely arrival of *these supplies saved those posts from inevitable destruction.* There being no transportation at Picolata, the Quartermaster procured four horses at Jacksonville for the purpose of forwarding one of the

* This gentleman has rendered such important services to his adopted country, as Quartermaster and Commissariat, that were I to omit the opportunity to express the high regard which is entertained for him in the American army, I should commit an act of injustice. Major Beard's business talents and gentlemanly deportment eminently fit him for those stations, and place him without an equal in the corps.

six pounders to Fort Drane, but when they arrived at the former place two of the horses were found unfit for service. A train of two small wagons, and ten chicken carts had fortunately been sent by General Hernandez for ammunition and arms for the defence of St. Augustine, and a council among the officers of the volunteers resulted in an order to the Quartermaster to *press* the mule teams into the service of the United States in transporting these necessaries to Fort Drane for the purpose of affording relief to the brave Clinch, whose supplies were exhausted. Accordingly the Richmond Blues, one hundred and twelve strong, with the Camden and Glynn mounted volunteers, numbering twenty-seven, and the Darien Infantry of about the same force, under their gallant commanders, Captains Robertson, R. [Richard] Floyd and T. [Thomas] Bryant, took up a line of march as an escort to the two six pounders, ordnance stores, and twenty-five wagons and carts laden with provisions, passing through the heart of the enemy's country, and arrived, on the 15th of February, without obstruction, amidst the cordial congratulations of the almost destitute garrison of Fort Drane. Supplies were immediately conveyed under the same escort to Fort King, which post was only saved from abandonment by their timely arrival. The Quartermaster's department was still very defective for the want of good transportation, and subsistence was also exceedingly scarce at these posts, in consequence of which the troops were put on three quarter rations. The Commissary of that post; (Lieutenant Dancy,) at great personal risk, was compelled to scour the neighbouring counties, and fortunately succeeded in procuring about ten thousand pounds of bacon, (half cured,) and one hundred bushels of meal.

The following are among the Georgia volunteer companies that subsequently arrived in Florida.

The Hancock Blues,	Capt.	A. S. Brown.
State Fencibles,	"	J. A. Meriwether.
Macon Volunteers,	"	Isaac Seymour.
Morgan Guards,	"	N. G. Foster.
Monroe Musqueteers,	"	John Cureton.
Washington Cavalry,	"	C. J. Malone.
Baldwin Cavalry,	"	W. F. Scott.

Several companies of well-appointed mounted men arrived from the same state under the brave and gallant Major Ross, but the lateness of the season prevented their entering the field, and they consequently returned much disappointed.

While desolation was stalking abroad, and the states of Georgia and South Carolina were endeavouring to check the career of the Seminole, Louisiana, the patriotic Louisiana was up and doing. The melancholy tidings of poor Dade's fate came upon them like a thunder bolt, and they could scarcely believe its reality. No time, however, was lost, but a meeting was forthwith called for the purpose of raising volunteers. At this moment, about the 15th of January, Maj. Gen. Gaines, who was on a tour of inspection through his (the western) Department,[*] first heard of the disturbances in Florida, when he

---

[*] The United States is divided into two great Military Departments, by a line drawn from the southern point of Florida, to the north-western extremity of Lake Superior. The Eastern department is under the supervision and control of Major. Gen. Scott, and the Western under that of Major Gen. Gaines. These departments are constituted for the convenience of the

immediately communicated with the Governor of Louisiana, and requested him to hold in readiness a body of volunteers for service in subduing the Seminole Indians. General Gaines then wrote to the adjutant General at Washington, urging that no time should be lost in succouring the troops in Florida, and declaring, from his knowledge of the Seminole character, that at least four thousand men would be required to subdue them, protected by a strong naval force. He recommended that officer to order the sixth and parts of the first and seventh regiments of infantry to Florida without delay. This done, he forthwith proceeded to Pensacola for the purpose of soliciting the co-operation of the naval forces on that station; but Commodores Dallas[94] and Bolton[95] and Capt. Webb[96] had already received orders to direct their attention to the inlets of Florida, whither they repaired. The alarming intelligence which met Gen. Gaines at Pensacola, induced him to adopt the most prompt and decisive measures to sustain the military posts

---

service; and by a reference to the map of the United States it will be seen that the line passes directly through the theatre of hostilities in Florida. The meeting of these two distinguished Generals was purely accidental. Gen. Scott was at Washington when the news of Gen. Clinch's battle with the Seminoles arrived. As the crisis demanded immediate action, and as Gen. Scott was present and could receive the instructions of the government in person, he was therefore charged with the direction of the campaign without regard to departmental boundaries. General Gaines had left his head quarters at Memphis, on a tour of inspection through his department, and it was very uncertain when or where the orders of the government would reach him, and as the services of an officer of high rank, of sound and discreet judgment, were required to maintain the neutrality of the United States during the war between the Texians [*sic*, but common at the time] and Mexicans, *he* (Gen. Gaines) was selected for that important post. But it appears that the official despatches did not reach Gen. Gaines until he had already taken the field in Florida, and had marched from Fort Brooke to Fort King, within ninety-five miles of where General Scott had established his head quarters.

within his command, and to secure peace to the frontier. On his arrival at Mobile, the 18th January, General Gaines heard that Fort Brooke was invested by the Indians, and the garrison in great danger of being cut off, which prompted him at once to send an express to General Clinch, then supposed to be at Fort King, stating that he should arrive at Fort Brooke about the eighth of February with seven hundred men, and requested General Clinch to take the field and march to the southward to form a junction with him (Gen. Gaines) at Fort Brooke. Lieut. Col. Twiggs[97] was then ordered to receive into service the eight companies of volunteers requested of the Governor of Louisiana, and with such regular troops as might be at the post in the vicinity of New Orleans, to hold himself in readiness for a movement to Tampa Bay. The enlistment of troops commenced on the 24th January, and on the third of February they were mustered into service. The General having arrived in New Orleans on the 27th, he chartered the steamers Merchant, Watchman and David Brown, to convey the troops and a quantity of subsistence, which he had taken the precaution to provide, to Fort Brooke. The Legislature of Louisiana in the most patriotic manner subscribed eighty-five thousand dollars for the equipment of the volunteers and purchase of subsistence, and, on the 4th February, at day light, the steamers Watchman and Merchant, on Lake Ponchartrain [sic], with the volunteers and one company of regulars, were underweigh for the afore-named post; and the same day the David Brown with Colonel Twiggs and companies B, E, G, H, I and K, of the regulars, left New Orleans for the same destination. Having put in at Pensacola and Apalachicola for supplies of fuel, the Merchant, Watchman and David Brown successively arrived in Hillsboro' Bay, about four miles distant, but within sight of the garrison, on the 8th, 9th and 10th of February, and the troops were immediately disembarked and bivouacked outside of the fort. This structure is a triangular work formed by pickets, with blockhouses at the apex, the base resting upon the bay, and flanked on the west side by the Hillsboro' river. On our arrival here, we found about two hundred regulars, composed of companies A, B, C and H, of second artillery, and company A of the fourth infantry, with Majors Belton, Zantzinger,[98] Mountfort, Lieutenants Grayson,[99] M'Kenzie,[100] Casey,[101] Legate,[102] Morgan,[103] Allen and Alvord,[104] and Doctors Heiskell[105] and Reynolds,[106] U. S. A.—the first named being the commanding officer of the post.

General Gaines having received instructions at Pensacola from the Secretary of War,[*] to repair and take charge of the forces which were assembling on the Mexican frontier, he announced the fact to Colonels Twiggs and Smith; but the troops on hearing of it manifested much dissatisfaction, and insisted that, as they had volunteered to go under the command of General Gaines, he should accompany them. Finding the current so strong in favor of his taking the field, as that period

---

[*] The following is extracted from the letter of the Secretary to General Gaines:—

War Department, Jan. 23, 1836.

"Sir—I am instructed by the President to request that you will repair to some proper position near the western frontier of the state of Louisiana, and there assume the personal command of all the troops of the United States which are or may be employed in any part of the region adjoining the Mexican boundary. It is not the intention of this order to change at all the relations between yourself and the military departments under your command, but to require your personal presence at a point where public considerations demand the exercise of great discretion and prudence."

was the most propitious for operating successfully, and the friendly Indians having been engaged the day before the arrival of the Louisiana troops, in a battle with the hostiles, about four miles from Fort Brooke, the General deemed it his duty to remain in the field until further advised by the War Department,* which he believed he might do with safety, as his services on the western frontier would not be required until late in March, if even then.

Accordingly, orders were issued from his head quarters, assigning the officers to their respective duties.—Captain Ethan A. Hitchcock[107] of the first infantry, was appointed Assistant Inspector General of the department, and Lieut. J. F. Izard[108] of the dragoons, to be Acting Brigade Major. The artillery and infantry of the United States, with the Louisiana forces under Adjutant General Persifor F. Smith,[109] were to constitute "the light brigade;" the whole to be commanded by Lieut. Colonel David E. Twiggs,** of the fourth infantry. The Louisiana volunteers were divided into two battalions—the first composed of the companies of Captains [Alexander] Burt, [J. G.] Lee, [J. W.] Williams, [W. A.] Rogers and [Hezekia] Thistle, under Lieut. Col. Lawson,[110] (surgeon U. S. A.;) the second, composed of the companies of Captains [Henry] Marks, [Croghan] Ker, [William] Magee, [Thomas] Smith, [Joseph] Abadie and [James] Barr, under Major [Samuel] Marks; the regiment to be commanded by Colonel Persifor F. Smith. Orders were issued thereto to prepare for a march on

---

* General Gaines was not at this time aware that General Scott had been ordered to Florida.

** This distinguished and brave officer has lately been promoted to the command of the new regiment of dragoons which has been organized since the adjournment of Congress. His loss to the fourth regiment of infantry will be most severely felt.

the 13th, supplied with forty rounds of ammunition and ten days' rations,[*] five of which to be carried in the haversacks of each man. Major Sands[111] of the fourth infantry, with those regulars that were unable to march, and Captain Barr's company of volunteers, amounting in all to about one hundred and sixty or seventy fighting men, were detailed for the protection of the fort, under command of the first named officer.

The order of march was in three columns, viz., a centre, supported by a right and left; each column equidistant one hundred yards, with a strong advance and rear guard to the centre column. The advance guard to move in single file, open order, preserving a distance of four feet between each man; the main or centre column, double file, open order—in the rear of which was the baggage train, supported by the rear guard in the same order. The right and left columns (or flankers) to move in the same manner as the advance guard, viz., single file, open order.

Centre column.—Composed of one company of volunteers as advance guard, under Brigade Major Izard; seven compa-

---

[*] The component parts of the ration are as follows:—Three-fourths of a pound of pork or bacon, or one and one-quarter pound of fresh or salt beef; eighteen ounces of bread or flour, or twelve ounces of hard bread, or one and one-quarter pound of corn meal, to each man, per day;—and at the rate of four pounds of soap, one and a half pounds of candles, two quarts of salt, four quarts of vinegar, eight quarts of peas or beans, four pounds of coffee, and eight pounds of sugar to each hundred men, per day. During the Florida campaign, the only articles drawn by the privates of the volunteer corps were bread or flour, pork or beef, and some few drew salt, sugar and coffee. The officers are of course enabled to draw the full rations in preference to the privates, where the supplies are, for instance, limited. The private is entitled to one ration a day, in value about eighteen or twenty cents; the officers, according to their rank or grade, are entitled to two, three, four, to eight rations a day. In case the rations are not drawn, the soldier or officer has the privilege of drawing its value in money.

nies of U. States artillery and infantry, under Lieut. Col. Foster;[112] the baggage train led by Capt. Shannon;[113] six companies of Louisiana volunteers, as rear guard, under Lieut. Col. Lawson.

Right column.—Four companies artillery, acting as light infantry, under Major Belton.

Left column.—Four companies Louisiana volunteers under Major Marks.

The whole command consisted of nine hundred and eighty effective men, exclusive of the detachment under Major Sands, which would swell the entire force at Fort Brooke, on the 12th February, to about eleven hundred and forty men. The Quartermaster's department at this post was in wretched condition, destitute of nearly every necessary; there were but about seventy horses, and they were in very bad condition. The ordnance stores were also defective, and the supplies very limited. Had the troops encountered the enemy on their march to Fort King, they must necessarily have laboured under very great disadvantages, as the powder used by the riflemen was of the most inferior description, and after two or three discharges, the gun became so clogged as to require cleaning. Of *subsistence* there was an abundance, and of good quality.

On the 13th of February the army was reviewed by Major General Gaines, and, accompanied by seventy-seven friendly Indians, they took up a line of march[*] towards the Alafia river, whither the General was informed that the body of hostiles, with whom the friendlies had been engaged a few days anterior, had gone. On this day great delay and trouble was experienced with the baggage train—horse after horse broke down,

---

[*] The course of the army of General Gaines is designated on the map, and his various encampments are marked by a cross.

and the men were obliged to burthen themselves still more. In consequence of this a considerable number of camp-kettles, spades, axes, &c., were buried.* Continuing the route until near dark, the army was brought to a halt about six miles from Fort Brooke, where they encamped. At dusk, the following day, they arrived at Warren's on the Alafia river, (eighteen miles from the fort,) where they received two days' rations, which the General had ordered to be sent around from Fort Brooke by water. Dicovering [*sic*] no traces of the Indians in that neighbourhood, the General deemed it his duty to direct a march towards the massacre ground of Major Dade and his brave band; and the boats having returned to Fort Brooke with the sick and disabled, and all superfluous baggage, the army moved on in the direction of a deserted Indian village, thence to pass the ruins of Simmonds' Howards, and Captain Sanders,' and strike the military road near the Hillsboro' river. On the 17th they arrived at the river and halted, preparatory to fording it, as the bridge was destroyed, and again resuming the line, accomplished fourteen miles. On the 18th they encamped, after burning two deserted villages near to the Big Ouithlacoochee, when the friendly Indians requested permission of the General to return to Fort Brooke. The General assured them, however, that there was no danger to be appre-

---

* These articles were subsequently discovered by the enemy and disinterred; but the brave and gallant Major (now Brigadier General) Leigh Read, having arrived at Fort Brooke a few days after General Gaines left, with two hundred and sixty volunteers from St. Marks, and hearing that a party of the hostiles were in the neighbourhood, he started at midnight on the 9th of March, and about six o'clock next morning attacked them; their dogs giving the alarm, they fled, leaving the kettles, spades, their rifles, blankets, and several ponies, which were secured by the Major.

hended; that he only required them to act as scouts and guides, and they need not enter into battle. With this assurance they concluded to continue with him. Both branches of the Ouithlacoochee were forded on the 19th, and that night a breastwork was thrown up around that which had been occupied on the 27th of December by the ill-fated party of Dade.

Resuming their march at daybreak on the 20th, they pursued the even tenor of their way until about nine o'clock, when the appearance of large flocks of vultures but too plainly foretold the approach of the army to the sad spot of slaughter. The advanced guard having passed the battle ground without halting, the General and his staff came upon one of the most appalling and affecting scenes that the human eye ever beheld. A short distance in the rear of the little field work lay a few broken cartridge boxes, fragments of clothing, here and there a shoe or an old straw hat, which perhaps had been exchanged for a military cap; then a cart partly burnt, with the oxen still yoked lying dead near it; a horse had fallen a little to the right, and here also a few bones of the hapless beings lay bleaching in the sun; while the scene within, and beyond the triangular enclosure, baffles all description. One would involuntarily turn aside from the horrible picture to shed a tear of sorrow, and 'wish that *he* had nothing known or nothing seen.' From the positions in which the bodies of this devoted little band were found, it was evident that they had been shot down in the faithful execution of their duty; their bodies were stretched with striking regularity nearly parallel to each other, and it is very doubtful whether the Indians touched them after the

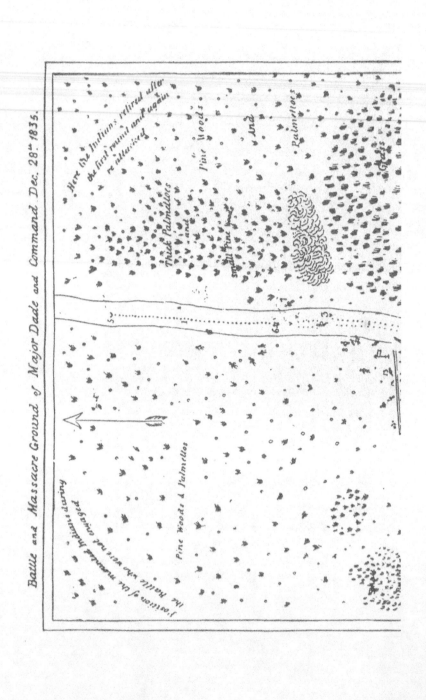

Battle and Massacre Ground of Major Dade and Command. Dec. 28th. 1835.

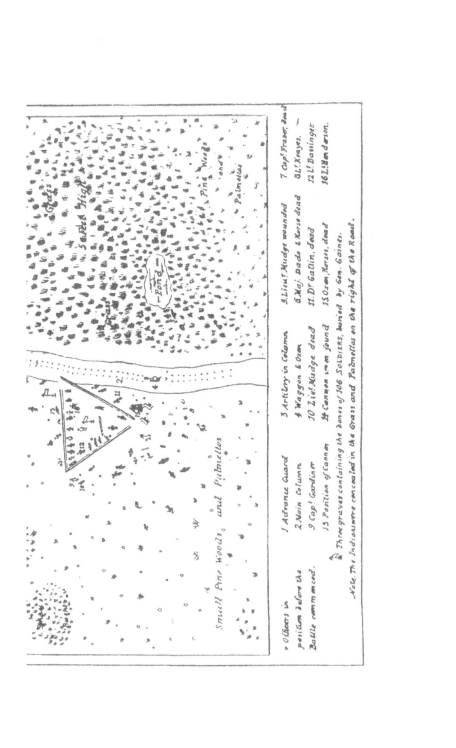

Small Pine Woods, and Palmettos

Grass

Scattered high

Pine Woods and Palmetto

—Pond—

1 Advance Guard
2 Main Column
9 Capt Gardiner
13 Position of Cannon

3 Artillery in Column
4 Waggon & Oxen
10 Lieut Mudge dead
14 Cannon were found

5 Lieut Mudge wounded
6 Maj: Dade & Horse dead
11 Dr Gatlin, dead
15 Oxen, Horses, dead

7 Capt Fraser, dead
8 Lt Keyes. —
12 Lt Basinger.
16 Lt Henderson.

⊹ Officers in
position before the
Battle commenced.

Three graves containing the bones of 106 SOLDIERS, buried by Gen. Gaines.

Note. The Indians were concealed in the Grass and Palmettos on the right of the Road.

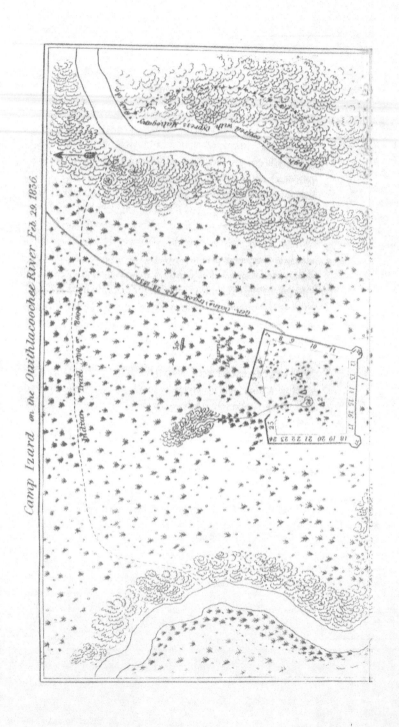

Camp Izard on the Ouithlacoochee River Feb. 29. 1836.

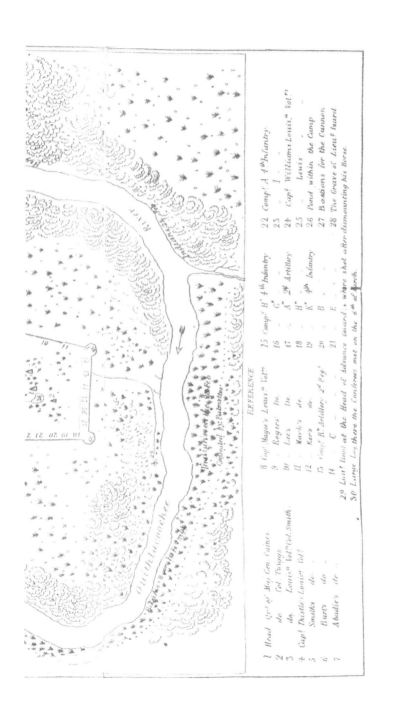

REFERENCE

1 Head Qrs of Maj. Gen. Gaines
2 do Col Twiggs
3 do Louisa Vol. Col. Smith.
4 Capt. Thistle's Louisa Vol.?
5 Smiths do
6 Butts do
7 Abadie's do

8 Capt Mage's Louis.a Vol.m
9 " Rogers' Do.
10 " Lee's Do.
11 " Marks's do.
12 " Kers do.
13 Comp.y B.a Artillery 2.d Reg.t
14 " C

15 Comp.y H.a 4.th Infantry
16 " G.
17 " A.a 2.d Artillery
18 " H.a
19 " K.a 4th Infantry
20 " B
21 " E

22 Comp.y A 4.th Infantry
23 " I
24 Capt. William.s Louis.a Vol.ry
25 " Lewis
26 Pond within the Camp
27 Bastions for the Cannon
28 The Grave of Lieut.t Izard

29 Lieut.t Izard at the Head of Advance Guard, where shot after dismounting his horse.
30 Large Log there the Contrees met on the 8.th of March.

battle, except to take some few scalps and to divest the officers of their coats. A short distance further, in the middle of the road, was the advanced guard, about twenty-eight in number, and immediately in the rear lay the remains of poor Dade, while a few feet to the right in the rear was that of the estimable Captain Fraser. To guard against surprise, our troops had been immediately formed into a quadrangular line, and soon after a detail of the regulars commenced the pleasing though mournful task of consigning the remains of their mutilated brethren in arms to whence they came. Within the enclosure two large graves were dug, into which the bodies of ninety-eight non-commissioned officers and privates were placed, and outside of the north-east angle of the work another grave received the bodies of eight officers, at the head of which, the field piece, which had been spiked and concealed by the enemy, but recovered, was planted vertically. The regular troops, formed into two columns and led by the immediate friends of the deceased officers, then moved, with reversed arms, in opposite directions, three times around the breastwork while the bands played the Dead March.

It now became a question of some importance with the General, whether he should continue his march to Fort King, which post he had been informed was besieged by the enemy, or return with his troops to Fort Brooke. To this latter post it was about sixty-five miles, and to the former forty miles, north. A large number of the volunteers were destitute of provisions—it would require five days to reach Fort Brooke, and but two to reach Fort King. The following reasons urged the General to move to the latter post.

Firstly.—It having been reported at Fort Brooke that Fort King was assailed by the Indians, and in danger of being cut off, and this opinion having been strengthened by the non-compliance of General Clinch with the request of General Gaines to co-operate with him, it became the duty of the latter to ascertain the cause.

Secondly.—The destitution of a large body of the volunteers.

Thirdly.—The Senior Assistant Quartermaster, Capt. Shannon, exhibited a letter from the Quartermaster General at Washington, dated the 19th January, which stated that "large supplies of provisions *had been* ordered from New York to Fort King," and which was ascertained to amount to one hundred and twenty thousand rations. These provisions having been shipped *before* the 19th January, according to the letter of Quartermaster Jesup, there could be no doubt that they had arrived at Fort King before the 20th of February,[*] a period of

---

[*] Orders were issued by the Commissary General of Subsistence, on the 6th and 8th of January, to the Acting Assistant Commissary at New York. On the 8th and 10th these communications respectively reached the Assistant. Now suppose these shipments were made one week, say seven days after the orders were received, (and if they were not, they should have been,) this will make the shipment from the date of *last* order, on the 17th of January. Now give *fifteen* days' passage to Picolata, which is a *very* long time, as vessels preform [sic] the trip to New Orleans, on *an average*, in that period, (and generally at that season in a shorter time,) and the provisions are landed at Picolata on the 1st of February. The longest period consumed in travelling between Picolata and Fort King, (ninety-two miles,) during the worst state of the roads, (but no rain had fallen since the preceding September, and the roads were in very good condition,) is about four and a half or five days—which would place these provisions at Fort King on the *5th of February!* Why were they not there? *Let the suffering army of Florida ask* MR. QUARTERMASTER GENERAL T. S. JESUP!

But to come at once to the true state of facts, these provisions were promptly shipped by the orders of the Commissary General, and were landed at Picolata, or were ready to land, about *the 28th of January.* The Quartermaster General Jesup, notwithstanding the urgency of the

more than thirty days. General Gaines therefore concluded that he would find supplies at that post; he might be enabled to ascertain the position of the enemy, and at the same time, if it was required, strengthen the garrison.

These considerations were sufficiently strong to prompt the advance upon Fort King, and, accordingly, orders were issued to take up the line of march. On the 22d of February the arrival of the army at Fort King was hailed by the small garrison, (about fifty men,) under Lieut. Col. Crane,[114] with enthusiastic delight. When the General approached, the guard was paraded, and the customary honours were paid in due form.

Finding that this post was badly supplied with subsistence, and indeed bare of every essential requisite to the prosecution of a war, the General directed Lieut. Col. Foster, with an escort of the fourth infantry, to proceed with the horses to Fort Drane, twenty-two miles north west, where General Clinch was stationed with four companies of artillery, one of infantry,

---

case, *grossly neglected to provide transportation to convey them to the suffering garrison, and they lay in the store house at Picolata until the 11th or 12th of February.* The indefatigable *volunteer* Quartermaster Beard, of the Richmond Blues, immediately pressed a number of horses, carts and wagons into the service, for the purpose of affording relief to the brave Clinch, and with a small escort arrived at Fort Drane in time to save that and the other military post from destruction!

The Commissary General of Subsistence is fully exonerated from any connexion [*sic*] with this delay; for, as far as I can learn, he has been prompt in complying with every requisition upon his department. It may be well to observe, that between the 6th of January and the 1st of April, about five hundred and fifteen thousand rations of pork, bacon, flour, bread and sugar, were ordered by the Commissary General to Florida—sufficient for the subsistence of one thousand men for five hundred and fifteen days, or for five thousand men, one hundred and three days. Any difficulty or delay which may occur in transporting provisions or stores of any description, must fall upon the Quartermaster, whose duty it is to provide the means of carriage.

and two companies of volunteers. The detachment returned
on the 24th with seven days' rations, accompanied by the generous and noble-hearted Clinch, and two companies of the
brave Georgians. It was here, *for the first time, that General
Gaines was informed that General Scott was in command in
Florida,* and was then at Picolata preparing force and supplies
to operate with;—hence his next movement was doubly important. To remain at Fort King was out of the question, as
supplies would be consumed as fast as they were brought, and
thereby materially embarrass the operations of General Scott;
and it was evident that the enemy would not be found by re-
tracing his steps to Fort Brooke—whereas, by moving in another direction, viz., by the battle ground of General Clinch,
even should he not succeed in meeting the enemy, the presence of a large force would, perhaps, tend to concentrate him,
and thereby give security to the frontier, and enable the inhabitants to return to their planting operations;—at all events he
would reach supplies at Fort Brooke, and, on his arrival there,
the army would give strength to the "wing," which was then
forming at that post under Col. Lindsay.[115] This latter course
was adopted upon much and mature deliberation, and preparations were accordingly made to move on the 26th. Taking two
days' rations, which were found at Fort King, with the seven
day's supplies received from Clinch, one six pounder drawn
by four horses, one four horse wagon, one cart and thirteen of
the friendly Indians, the army took up the line of march at day
light, and encamped about twenty miles distant. On the 27th,
at two o'clock, having still preserved the same order of march,
they struck the river at three points, the advance guard of the

centre column being at the usual crossing place. A halt was sounded, and, leaving the baggage train protected by the rear guard, the General, with the main column and artillery, moved forward for the purpose of making a personal reconnoisance [*sic*] preparatory to crossing. Finding the river too deep and the current very strong, General Gaines, accompanied by Col. Smith, made an attempt to ford about two hundred and fifty yards higher up. When they reached a small island in the middle of the river, a very sharp and spirited fire was opened upon them, accompanied by the enlivening war yell of the savage. The volunteers and regulars returned the compliment, but as the enemy were much shielded by the underbrush, the field piece, under Lieut. Grayson, was brought to bear upon them, when a few well-directed and destructive canisters[*] quickly silenced their yelling. The engagement lasted about three quarters of an hour, during which one volunteer was killed and seven wounded, when the enemy having ceased firing, the General ordered the men to retire from the river. The breastwork occupied by Gen. Clinch in December, situated about half a mile from the Ouithlacoochee, was enlarged, and the command encamped for the night. The four bodies which were buried by Gen. Clinch, after his battle, had been disinterred and scalped by the Indians; Gen. Gaines ordered them reburied.

The friendlies informed the General, that a few miles lower down he would find a more open country, with pine barren

---

[*] For the information of those who are not acquainted with military epithets, I beg leave to explain:—They are tin cases filled with various sizes of iron balls from an ounce to five or six ounces in weight, and when the gun is discharged the canister bursts, and these balls are scattered in as many different directions as they number.

woods, and less hammocky along the banks; this information determined General Gaines to move in that direction. Accordingly, at daybreak on the 28th, the line was again formed, and after a circuitous march of four miles, (two miles in a direct line,) the advanced guard arrived at the crossing place. Major Izard, mounted, was about forming the guard on the right of the trail, when the sharp crack of a rifle, and the war yell gave notice of the presence of the enemy, and he discovered that his horse had received the ball in his neck. Immediately dismounting and securing his horse in the rear of a near hammock, he repaired to the bank of the river, and discovering that his men were unable to command the other bank, he went on in front to inspire them, when he received a ball which grazed his right eye, passing into the inner corner, destroying the ethmoid bone, running back of the left eye, then out in the near of the temple. He immediately dropped; but, partially recovering himself, he heroically ordered, "Keep your positions, men, and lie close."[*] The battle continued with a slight intermission from nine o'clock to one, P. M., when the firing

---

[*] First Lieut. James Farley Izard belonged to the dragoons, but being on leave of absence he volunteered his services to Maj. Gen. Gaines, and was appointed by him Acting Brigade Major. He survived this desperate wound five days, during which time he underwent the most intense suffering. When the firing commended on the 2d of March, it was difficult to restrain him from getting up; on one occasion he made a violent effort to leap from his bed, but sunk down exhausted before he succeeded in crossing the little frame which had been thrown up around his tent. A few hours before his spirit departed, he remarked, "It is very hard! I am the last of my family, and to die *such* a death!" He visited the General's tent the morning on which he was shot, and he seemed very much depressed. The loss of Lieut. Izard was deeply felt and mourned by the Louisianians, as he had imparted to them many useful lessons in military exercise—aside from his mild and gentlemanly bearing towards them, which endeared him to all.

He was buried on the 5th of March, in the east bastion of the camp, named in honour of him by General Gaines; a stately and venerable oak overshadows the grave, and every precaution was adopted to conceal it

and yelling on the part of the enemy ceased. The troops were accordingly withdrawn and formed in a quadrangular line, around which they threw up a breastwork, the near front resting about one hundred and twenty yards from the river. Besides Lieut. Izard, Capt. Sanders, commanding friendly Indians, was severely wounded; Capt. Armstrong, of the U. States transport schooner Motto, slightly; and one private of Capt. Croghan Ker's company of Louisiana volunteers, killed.

At ten o'clock, P. M., General Gaines sent an express of ten mounted men, under the gallant and meritorious Lieut. Edw'd M'Dermott, of the Bayou Sara volunteers, with despatches to Gen. Clinch, requesting that officer to co-operate with him by crossing the river eight or ten miles above, and come down upon the enemy's rear. He also stated that he would not remove from his position until he heard from General Clinch, and requested to be furnished with six thousand rations of pork, flour and sugar, with a small assortment of Quartermaster's stores, viz., saws, adzes, augurs, spikes, nails, &c., necessary for the formation of a bridge—and one six-pounder, with an assortment of shot, and ten thousand musket cartridges.

The express arrived at Fort Drane, unmolested, about five o'clock on the following morning; when another was despatched by General Clinch to General Scott, at Picolata.

---

from the researches of the Indians. It is gratifying to state, that the grave remained untouched on the 29th of March, when Generals Scott and Clinch passed the consecrated spot.

On the 29th orders were issued for one-third of the command to remain on watch inside of the encampment, while one third was engaged in strengthening the defences; a detachment of two hundred of the Louisiana volunteers, under the expert marksman and most excellent officer, Capt. Thistle, was detailed for the erection of a blockhouse near the river, while others were engaged in preparing canoes, &c. Every thing went on quietly until about ten o'clock, when the working parties were fired upon, and simultaneously a heavy volley of at least one thousand guns poured into three sides of the encampment,* the one nearest the river being the only one not assailed. Numbers of the enemy, concealed by the palmettos and small bushes on every side of the work, came so near that they wounded the troops on the opposite side of the camp, a distance of two hundred yards. Finding that they could not induce the General to leave his position, the enemy set fire to the grass and palmettos with a view to burn the breastwork down, but suddenly the wind shifted and carried the destruction towards themselves. The firing continued with unabated fury for two hours, when the enemy retired, and as the men were instructed by the General in person not to expend their ammunition unless "you can see the white of your enemy's eye," it is presumable that their loss must have been heavy. The bugle sounded a *retreat*, when the working party, under

---

* Camp Izard was about two hundred yards square, and from a calculation made by the officers best acquainted with the service, and the opinions of the friendly Indians, the enemy were estimated to have been *fifteen hundred strong*. One of the friendly chiefs furnished Capt. Hitchcock with a list of the war chiefs, with their respective commands of warriors, and they amount to one thousand and sixty *without* the negroes, and the accessions which they have doubtless had since the war began, from the Creeks.

Capt. Thistle, returned to camp without suffering any loss; but the brave Captain was of opinion that the enemy suffered very much from his little party, they having concealed themselves in the hammock until the Indians came up close to them without knowing that *their* enemy was for fighting them in *their* way—when Captain Thistle ordered *"fire,"* and many were observed to fall. The Captain is a man of strict veracity, and he assured the General *he* "had a *bead* upon three." A small party then went out for the purpose of reconnoissance, when they discovered that the enemy, in their haste to retreat, had left one of their dead upon the field, who was found a short distance from the work and brought in—his skull having been quartered and carried away by a canister shot; he was an elderly Indian and we found him plentifully supplied with the *finest* quality of rifle powder, fifty or sixty small bullets, two lady's silver thimbles, a spool of cotton, an ivory lace point, an ostrich feather and a variety of other *nic nacks.* About four o'clock, P. M., they again fired on the camp, but were obliged to keep at a respectful distance from our sharp-shooters, as their attempt to burn the camp ended in destroying their own means of concealment. The troops fired but seldom, as the Indians were so far off as to preclude the possibility of dropping them.[*] Finding that their efforts were fruitless, one of the chiefs with a stentorian voice called to them, "come off; never

---

[*] Not that the distance was too great for the gun to cast its *load*, but the Yager or United States rifles are very *inaccurate*, and cannot be depended upon in shooting at long distances. The U. S. rifles will throw a ball nearly four hundred yards, but even in the hands of a good marksman he will find it difficult to hit a man at one hundred and twenty yards. The Indian rifles are generally much more accurate.

mind, boys, when they go to cross the river we'll give them scissors"—a horn was then sounded and the enemy retired. During the day the loss in camp was one serjeant [*sic*] of artillery, killed; and thirty-two officers, non-commissioned officers and privates, wounded. Among the latter was the gallant hero himself, who received a small ball in the lower lip which forced a front tooth from its socket; in the most cheerful manner he responded to the expressed sympathies of those near him. "Oh, it is no-thing, though it was very unkind in the enemy to take a tooth from me, and one that I valued so highly;" also Lieut. Duncan[116] of the 2d artillery; Mr. W. Potter,[117] secretary to the General, and Lieut. Ephraim Smith of the Louisiana volunteers, who received three wounds.

Another express by three of the friendly Indians was sent this night to General Clinch, advising him of the temerity of the enemy in attacking us in our position, and his supposed force, and recommending that General to march the forces under his command direct to Camp Izard instead of crossing the river above. He was also requested to procure, if possible, a few hundred mounted men, even if it should require some days to collect them; to forward one or two field pieces, one hundred and fifty rounds of canister and fifty rounds of grape shot, ten thousand musket ball and buckshot cartridges, some corn for the horses, and repeating the request to be furnished with six thousand rations of pork, flour and sugar, a few light wagons or carts to carry his sick and wounded, and the Quartermaster's stores previously mentioned.

The General believed this opportunity to be too favourable to be lost; he only required provisions and stores to enable him to follow them up, and was confident that if he could secure the co-operation of the forces under Gen. Clinch, or *have the supplies* that he requested, that the war would be ended in ten days. The enemy were chuckling at the idea of cooping him up, and were *then concentrated,* and *that was the proper period to make a decisive blow* and close the war. But had General Gaines the means wherewith to do it?—He had not a saw, an adze, an augur, a spike, a nail, a rope, or any thing else to construct a bridge to cross his field piece, wagon and carts. Could he pass his army in a canoe, when the enemy were strewn along the banks for nearly two miles, without excessive risk in losing one-half of his men? One field-piece was insufficient to cover the crossing. Look at the instance of Gen. Clinch, in December preceding—how many men passed the river after the Indians became aware that their enemy was near?—ask Gen. Call, and the other brave officers "who, at imminent hazard, crossed the river during the battle!"—They will tell you that nearly five hundred volunteers were prevented from crossing in consequence of the Indians being concealed along the banks of the river, who picked off every man that attempted to get into the canoe. If it had been an open country, the case would have been different

Some ask, *why* was not a *sortie* made? If any man of ordinary understanding will for a moment reflect, he will perceive the most substantial reasons why: In the first place, Gen. Gaines, in his earliest letter to Gen. Clinch, sent by the express of the 28th of February, *prior* to any attack being made on the camp, says—"I shall abstain from making a *sortie* or moving from my position until I hear from you. In the mean time will endeavour to keep the enemy amused whilst I am preparing canoes, boats, &c., preparatory to crossing, until the forces under your command can be brought to co-operate from the other side of the river." In his second letter, sent on the evening of the 29th, after the attack, he says—"Being fully satisfied that I am in the neighbourhood of the principal body of the Indians, and that they are now concentrated, I must suggest to you the expediency of an immediate co-operation with the forces under your command. I have only to repeat my determination, *not to move from my position, or make a sortie until I hear from you,* as it would only tend to disperse the enemy, and we should then have difficulty in finding him." But suppose, for a moment, that Gen. Gaines had directed a charge upon the enemy, and he had, as he certainly would have, lost one or two hundred of his men—what means had he of conveying his wounded, in case he should find it necessary to make a retreat thereafter? He had one wagon and two carts, sufficient perhaps for ten men, and he then had *forty* already wounded! No man would dare lay the charge of *fear* at his feet; for let them look upon the glorious page which records the noble daring of the *sortie at FORT ERIE*[*], and ask themselves if *ten thousand* yelling savages could overawe the veteran, where the honour of his country—sacred to him as life—was jeopardized! Such an accusation would stain its author an ungrateful maligner of the blackest dye, and undeserving the name of an American. Again—what advantage would have

---

[*] The sortie of Gen. Gaines at Fort Erie, was made on the 15th of August, 1814, and the British "acknowledged a *greater loss* then any they sustained on land during the war, prior to the battle of New Orleans, the 8th January, 1815."

been derived from a sortie, unless the enemy could have been followed up? Look at the case of Maj. Cooper,[118] with the Georgia battalion at Camp Cooper;—notwithstanding he made a sortie on the enemy whenever he appeared, yet they continued to harass him for thirteen successive days. So it would have been with Gen. Gaines, and having no means of following them up, they would have returned, and by this annoyance reduced his force and given him no corresponding advantage over them. Gen. Gaines doubtless never expected to have found the whole of the Indians imbodied [*sic*]; but finding them so it was very desirable and it was his greatest aim, to keep them together until, by one decisive blow, the war should be finished. It is true that the troops suffered much from hunger—but did the humane and gallant General *force* them to submit? No! here it is recorded, to be the admiration of the wise and discreet of every section, and to the glory of the republic, that not a man murmured. *All cheerfully and voluntarily consented* to sustain themselves upon the meat of their horses, in preference to abandoning such an important position, until the co-operation of Gen. Clinch could be secured. They had about thirty horses, which would have afforded them subsistence for *three weeks longer*!

On the first of March, at ten o'clock, the enemy again attacked us, but in smaller force, and after losing a few of their men, without doing us damage, they retired.—During the day the troops were still kept employed in preparing canoes and materials for the bridge. These friendly Indians left the camp about nine o'clock, with duplicate of the despatches to Gen. Clinch, which were directed to the commanding officer at Fort King.

On the 2d, the enemy, with a punctiliousness and etiquette which he does not always manifest, again visited us at *ten* o'clock, with a force nearly equal to that of the 29th February. The attack was very vigorous, and continued for an hour and a half, when one of the chiefs called to his men—"let us go and get dinner, and give them more before the sun goes down." They then retired, having wounded but three of our men very slightly.* About five o'clock, P. M., as the guard were forming, they re-appeared and fired a few shots without doing any mischief. They endeavoured to imitate our bugle several times with a horn which they had.

At daylight on the third, they fired about fifty shots into the camp, and a few stragglers would, occasionally through the day, creep up, fire and retreat. At about three o'clock, P. M., nearly six hundred of the Indians, divided into two detachments, each preceded by an ensign bearing a red flag, filed from the right and left in opposite directions, and countermarched like regular troops; they had a horn, (whether a bugle, tin trumpet, or cow's horn, we could not tell,) with which they made a horribly discordant noise; we also discovered

---

* This is no doubt owing to the careless manner in which the Indians sometimes load. Their first fire is generally dangerous, as the rifle is well loaded and the bullet patched. But when the Indian enters into battle, he fills his mouth with bullets, guesses at the quantity of powder, and the bullet is then dropped from the mouth into the barrel without a patch, and, hitting the butt a tap or two, he is ready to shoot again.—These shots cannot, of course, be effective, and hence it is that many of our men who were wounded on the 29th of February, received the shot from the rear, the bullet having passed by the object to which it was directed and gone to the other side of the camp, whilst others struck the trees in the enclosure as high as twenty and thirty feet. This is in consequence of the large charge of powder, which makes the bullet fly wild. Too little powder drives the bullet with more precision, but not so far.

several negroes with soldiers' clothing on. Many of the volunteers, belonging to the companies of Captains Lee, Burt, Magee, Abadie and a few others, were, from their excessive improvidence, again destitute of provisions—some having exhausted their rations[*] two days previous—the General therefore directed the distribution of some horse meat to the needy. Accordingly two horses were selected and apportioned among them, and much to the astonishment of those who had never before been necessitated to taste it, the horse meat was found to be deliciously flavoured; a small piece of the liver was cooked and brought by Capt. Thistle to Gen. Gaines, who seemed to relish it very well. The writer of these lines was also induced to partake of it, and, unless he had been told, he could not have detected the difference between it and a beef's liver.

About sunrise on the fourth, an attack was made upon several of the men who had gone outside for the purpose of procuring wood, and two of them were wounded; one man was killed inside of the camp. A guard was detailed at nine o'clock, under command of Capt. Thistle, who was instructed to proceed with the horses a short distance from the camp to fodder them; he returned without being molested, about three o'clock, A. M. This night the men were occasionally annoyed by a few straggling shots, which, however, did no damage.

---

[*] No volunteer corps should ever enter the service of the U. States, or go abroad, without appointing a Commissary and Quartermaster. The inconvenience and difficulty attendant on the distribution of each man's share, and the loss in cooking the provisions in small messes of one, two and three, would be remedied by the management of such officers.—Those companies that were organized with a Commissary, &c., to take charge of their stores, and one cook to supply all in one mess, were found with supplies on hand, while the others, who cooked their provisions in separate messes, were starving.

During the fifth, the enemy again threw away their powder and balls, for although they frequently fired, not a man was touched. As the guard were assembling at five o'clock they made an attack from a near hammock, where a few had concealed themselves, but their shots proved ineffectual. About seven o'clock in the evening the enemy commenced to build fires along the trail which they had formed, about four hundred yards in the rear of our camp. Having made three, at a distance of fifty yards from each other, as the fourth was lighting up, they were all suddenly extinguished. This, of course, excited our astonishment, and we knew not what to make of it. At ten o'clock a voice was heard at a great distance in the rear of the camp, but being very inarticulate, and supposing it to be news from General Clinch, the captain of the guard requested the stranger to "come nearer." Having come within hailing distance, the following dialogue ensued. Presuming the voice was Abraham's, his name will be used:—

Abraham.—Hallo, there!

Capt. of Guard.—What do you want?

Abr'm.—How far are your sentinels posted out?

Capt.—You can come up nearer, they shall not fire on you.

Abr'm.—(*Advancing within one hundred yards.*) Is Colonel Twiggs there?

Capt.—Yes!

Abr'm.—Tell him we don't want to fight him any more, and as to-morrow is a good day[*] we'll come in and shake hands, and be good friends.

Capt.—Very well, if you will come with a white flag you shall not be harmed.

---

[*] This interview, it will be remembered, is on Saturday night, 5th of March,

Abr'm.—We'll come in after breakfast to-morrow morning, about nine o'clock.—Good night.

The stranger retired, and while we were speculating upon the consequences of this strange interview, he again broke in upon the awful stillness which pervaded our camp—"As to-morrow is a good day, we hope you won't do any work or cut down any trees." The captain of the guard replied—"Very well." Gradually, all became hushed for the night, save the inaudible whisperings and light tread of those who waked in turn,

> To guard the camp from foe or flame;
> Around the smothered watch fires dim,
> "No warrior yell nor battle hymn,
> Upon the breeze of midnight came."

Our General, however, impressed on the minds of all to observe the greatest caution to prevent surprise. At *reveillie* the next morning, the troops were harangued by their commanders, and it was strictly enjoined upon them to be doubly watchful at their posts. Every man was required to keep his place at the breastwork with his musket or rifle in hand; the enemy might be intentionally honest, or he might be prepared to make a desperate, though it would to them have been a fatal, charge upon the works.

---

about ten o'clock. General Clinch moved from Fort Drane that same day, at twelve o'clock, and did not reach us until five o'clock the day following, (Sunday,) and it is evident that the Indian runners must have announced the movement of Gen. Clinch before seven o'clock Saturday evening—the distance is thirty two miles. This fact goes to show that the Indians have their spies always on the alert, and watch every movement of our army; by which means they know when to oppose, and when to step aside, and let the troops pass on.

At about half past eight o'clock on Sunday morning, the sixth of March, we espied the enemy of yesterday emerging simultaneously from the right and left of the hammocks,[*] the two detachments moving towards each other in their usual marching order, with a large dirty white flag; and having formed themselves opposite in the rear of our camp, the Adjutant of the Louisiana volunteers, Major [Albert] Barrow, volunteered to go out and ascertain their object. Having mounted a stump a few yards from the camp, the Major waved a white handkerchief, but the slow advance of Abraham gave evidence of his fears that he would be entrapped. The General having directed the interpreter, Mr. Hagan, to accompany Major Barrow, and listen to what was said by the Indians, the two took post about one hundred yards from the camp, and seated themselves on a log, (*see sketch of camp,*) when Abraham, accompanied by Jumper, moved cautiously towards them. A few minutes after they assembled, Dr. Harrall and Captain Marks of the volunteers, were granted permission to join the conferees, when Assiola and Coi Hajo appeared on part of the Indians. During the conference another left our camp, and was met by Caesar[119] (a black) from the opposite quarter. Thus they exhibited the greatest tenacity to have an equal representation; though it is most probable that this arose from fear that we would deal unfairly with them.

Major Barrow then asked them what they had to communicate. Jumper replied, through Abraham, that they wanted to stop fighting; that they had spilled much blood; that they had had revenge enough, (this Assiola approved of by an

---

[*] See the map of Camp Izard.

affirmative nod, and saying, *chor!*)—that they had taken up arms against the white people because they had been badly treated by them—that we had killed many of their men—that they would stop killing white men if we would withdraw our men and not cross the river; and that if we would remain on one side, they would go over and remain on the other. Major Barrow replied, that he would communicate their wishes to General Gaines. Jumper then asked if *Colonel Twiggs* did not command. The Major replied, that Colonel Twiggs was in camp, but that General Gaines was the *commanding officer.* Jumper said, he knew General Gaines very well; that he was a very kind and humane man, and he would like to have a talk with him. The conferees then returned to their respective parties, and were to meet again in half an hour.

Captain Hitchcock (one of the staff officers) was authorized by General Gaines to confer with Jumper, and he was accompanied by Captain Marks, Dr. Harrall, Mr. Hagan, and a soldier who knew Assiola at Fort King, while he was confined in irons. The time having expired, the parties again met, when Assiola advanced to shake hands with this man,[*] Chamberlain. Another gentleman having left the camp to join the confer-

---

[*] A great variety of stories have been concocted out of this interview, which have been greedily received as the truth, and bandied about in most of the newspapers throughout the country. For instance, "Powel asked Gen. Gaines if he was not hungry—come over the river and we'll give you two beeves and a bottle of brandy." "General Clinch is coming to your aid with five hundred horsemen;"—and that Powell said to Chamberlain, that "friends will meet in times of war as well as peace." And the last *manufacture* has appeared in a late publication, saying that "Oceola anxiously enquired after Lieutenant John Grahame, and on being informed that he was wounded, stoutly denied it. On being asked why he was so positive that Lieutenant Grahame was unhurt, he replied, that he had imperatively ordered his people never to molest that young man, and he knew no one who

ences, another chief, Holata Mico, approached, making the number of each party equal. Chamberlain having retired, the last named chief also returned to his men. Captain Hitchcock then stated to Jumper, that he was instructed by General Gaines to say, that he was not authorized to make a treaty with him—that having heard that they had been committing hostilities upon the white people of Florida, he came with his men to subdue them—that they must obligate themselves to cease killing the whites—retire to the south side of the Ouithlacoochee river, and remain there peaceably until the United States government sent commissioners to meet them in council and provide for their removal—that a large force was coming to operate against them, and every Indian that was found with a rifle in his hand would be shot down.

Jumper replied—*We know* that you have many men marching towards us, but our people are opposed to going away from the lands of their fathers; we were sorry that white people forced us to fight them, but they oppressed us and deprived us of our rights, and we could not bear it. We would like to see General Gaines and talk with *him* upon the subject.

Captain Hitchcock told Jumper that if they would go to the

---

would dare disobey him; none should, and live!" The author deems it his duty to disabuse the public ear of such trash, and will settle it in a few words. In the first place, Assiola, or Powel, does not speak the English language; and, in the second place, he spoke to no one except the interpreter, (who was busily engaged with Captain Hitchcock and Jumper) and his own people. When he shook hands with Chamberlain he unintelligibly muttered a few words in his own language, and smiled. In respect to the last story, I have been informed that it grew out of a little jest of the Lieutenant. It certainly is likely that the Indians would *select* their *men* on a field of battle! But to make a long story short—no such assertions were made by Assiola at the interview between the parties on the 6th of March.

camp they should see him, but this they refused to do.

Jumper said they would like to consult their governor, Miconopy, and know his views—that they had not seen him on the subject—that he was now some distance off, but had promised to be with them two or three days ago, and they did not know the reason of his delay.

Abraham asked Mr. Hagan where Captain Sanders was; and, to deceive them a little, Mr. Hagan replied that he was not with us; that he did not know where he was. Assiola exultingly and quickly remarked to Abraham—"I told you he was dead—I saw him fall."

During this and the first interview, Assiola, Alligator and Caesar, amused themselves with playful remarks and jests, which were fully understood by our interpreter, who had cautiously preserved his *incognito,* when, at this moment, he was very inconsiderately exposed by the doctor, with the remark, "this is our interpreter." The course of conversation was immediately changed, and Alligator asked Mr. Hagan how many men we had—He replied, that we had more than they. "No you have not," said Jumper—"We have two hundred here, (pointing to the party in the rear,) one hundred there, and one hundred there, (pointing to the right and left hammocks;) five hundred over there (pointing to the opposite side of the river,) and seven hundred with Miconopy. At this period one of the volunteers had gone out for wood and commenced to cut down a tree; the instant the noise was heard, the Indian broke off in his speech, and requested that the work might be stopped. Jumper continued—"It is difficult for us to restrain our young men, and we ordered them not to cross the river yesterday; but some of them are very weak and foolish, which gave us much sorrow when we heard that they had disobeyed our request."

One of the party asked Abraham, if they had lost many of their men. The question being interpreted to Jumper, he told Abraham to say, that out of his company of one hundred and sixty men, he had eight killed and five wounded. The negro, however, only said, that they had lost a good many; but our interpreter understood every word that was said.

Captain Hitchcock asked* Jumper if *Miconopy* was in any of the battles. Jumper replied, that he was over the river on the first day they crossed on this side, and that he left them the next day and promised to return in two days; they would like to see him before they gave a decisive answer. Captain Hitchcock replied, that there was no time to be lost, and that if they intended to surrender, they had better do so at once. Jumper asked for two days time to enable them to see Micanopy and have a talk with him, but Captain H. persisted in closing it at once. Finding that a dictation of terms would not avail, they agreed to go and hold a council and meet again before the sun went down. They again requested a talk with General Gaines; but Captain H. told Jumper that if Miconopy would come, General Gaines would meet *him*, as the Governor of the nation, or if they would go to the camp they could see him. After a short pause, Jumper asked if we had any brandy or

---

* I wish to be distinctly understood, that when I say, "asked Jumper," or any other of the chiefs, except negroes, the question was proposed to him *through* the interpreter, Abraham; and so with those chiefs' replies, as none of them speak English.

tobacco. Captain H. replied, that our brandy was out, but he thought he could furnish them with some tobacco. The conferees then parted to meet "before the sun goes down."

At half past four o'clock the Indians were seen emerging from the opposite extremities of the hammocks, and, as in the morning, arranged themselves in the rear of the camp. Some time after our conferees had assembled at the talking spot, the Indians moved slowly towards us. Jumper then said that they had talked with their people, but they were not willing to go to the west—that all were anxious to see Miconopy, and to know his views—that their people wished to have the Ouithlacoochee river as the dividing line between them and the white people. Captain Hitchcock said, in the most imperative and distinct manner, that General Gaines had no authority to make a treaty with them—that he only exacted from them a pledge that they would cease murdering the white people, and plundering their lands—that they must give up their arms, and retire to the south side of the river, and hold themselves in readiness to meet the United States commissioners in council whenever sent for.

After a little hesitation, they agreed that, for themselves and their men, they would sign an agreement to cease hostilities against the whites—to remain on the south side of the river—to give up their arms—and meet the commissioners in council whenever called upon.

At this moment we heard the report of two guns at a distance, when the Indians shewed [*sic*] great agitation, and said that they would come after breakfast in the morning to the landing on the river, with a white flag, and they hoped that General Gaines would come and talk with them. The Indians in the rear then gave a whoop, and commenced running to the right and left, when the friendlies, who were coming along with General Clinch, opened with a round yell and were ready for action.—Captain Hitchcock requested the chiefs to retire as soon as possible, and, after presenting them with two pounds of tobacco, which three of the Louisiana officers generously proffered, they took to their heels and were soon out of reach of the guns which Clinch's van guard discharged at them. Not knowing the object of the Indians being so near the camp, the line was formed immediately and an assault made.

The express of ten men, which left our camp on the 28th of February, were now returned, in company with the brave Georgians under Captains Robertson and [Samuel] Bones, the Florida mounted militia, headed by Major M'Lemore, and a few regulars under Captains Thruston[120] and Graham—the whole commanded by the soldier's friend, the gallant Clinch, who had moved to supply our craving appetites as soon as the militia could be collected to strengthen the escort. He furnished us with forty head of cattle, and two days' rations of hard bread, pork and sugar. The scene which ensued *beggars* all description. The half-starved Louisianians were like a flock of hungry wolves, scarcely giving the new comers time to get off their haversacks or canteens; but it afforded Georgians, Floridians and all, the greatest delight to feed the hungry—they parted with the last crumb—with the last drop.

General Clinch's command encamped in the rear of us— the north line of our defence dividing the two camps.

At about eight o'clock this evening, Abraham's voice was heard upon the other side of the river, asking for a postponement of the meeting until Tuesday, at 4 o'clock, P. M. Captain Hitchcock replied, that they must adhere to their promise, and appear at the landing at the stated time. They again asked, if they could talk with Gen. Gaines—but were told that, if Miconopy would be there, General Gaines could be spoken with. Having agreed to meet in the morning at the appointed hour, no more was heard of them that night. Failing in their engagement, on Monday morning many of our men, who were on the banks of the river anxiously awaiting a call from them, were persuaded to indulge themselves—some in fishing, whilst others dashed into the dark brown current, nor fearing to cross and tread the Seminole ground. Throughout the day the bank was lined with our men engaged in various pleasures.

On Tuesday morning the 8th, a negro by name of *Primus*, who had a wife among the hostile Indians, was sent among them, to account for his appearance in what manner he might think proper, with such instructions for his government as were deemed necessary.

On Wednesday the 9th, Gen. Gaines thought proper to deliver the command over to Gen. Clinch, who, for reasons assigned in his orders, directed the troops to prepare for a movement the next morning at ten o'clock. A heavy rain fell this night, which literally inundated both camps. That occupied by the Georgians was, in some places, eight or twelve inches deep, and hence its name—Camp *Misery.*

At twelve o'clock on Thursday the 10th, our line was formed, and soon on its way towards Fort Drane. The sick and wounded suffered very much on the road, from the manner in which they were crowded into the wagons, and it was pleasing to observe the solicitude manifested by the veteran Gaines, who dismounted from his horse and insisted upon its being taken by one of the young soldiers who was enfeebled from illness, while the General waded through swamp, and walked the whole distance, nearly seven miles, to our next encampment.—Having halted at six o'clock, we were gratified by the appearance of *Primus* among us. The negro found that the Indians had moved a few miles higher up the river, and he confirmed in every particular the sincerity of their professions. He was received by them in the most cordial manner, and when about to leave them they took his hand and bade him farewell—said that they were tired of war, and wished for peace, but they were unwilling to leave the country—that many of their men had been killed—that they had seen our people fishing and swimming in the river, but they ordered their young men not to fire upon them. *Primus* had been instructed to say to the Indians, that when Gen. Clinch's men fired upon them he did not know they were holding a conference with Gen. Gaines. They replied to this, that they knew it was a mistake—that two of *their* men had accidentally fired off their rifles while running, but they took no aim to do them injury.

On the 11th, at 7 o'clock, we resumed our march, and arrived at Fort Drane early in the afternoon. The Louisiana volunteers arrived about dark, and encamped three miles distant, at Camp Smith. The regulars took post at Camp Twiggs, about one mile east.

Upon transferring the command to Gen. Clinch, sixty-two officers of the second artillery, fourth infantry, and Louisiana volunteers, united in a letter of respect to Gen. Gaines, expressive of the high regard in which they held him as the soldier and gentleman, with their regrets that he was about to leave them. The General returned his thanks to the gallant and brave officers by whom he had been so manfully sustained, and said:

"The unsought approbation of such officers, highly acceptable to me at any time, is more especially so at the present moment, when the propriety of my movement is about to be questioned by those who would seem to sit still and amuse themselves with metaphysical abstractions founded upon European systems of tactics!—or by those irresponsible champions of intrigue and spirit of party who presume to *interfere with,* if they do not yet venture to *control,* every measure of every man who dares to think and to act honestly and faithfully, as we are bound by our oaths and honour to do.

"Whilst I continue to be honoured as I have been by the approbation of such men as [Presdient] Madison, and [Gen. Jacob] Brown,[121] and [Gen. Peter B.] Porter,[122] and White, and Twiggs, and Smith, and others who have served with me, witnessed my conduct and cordially sustained me as each one of you have, I cannot fail to maintain towards every assailant the attitude of honest defiance!"

General Gaines left Fort Drane with a small escort of mounted men on the 14th of March, for Tallahassee, where he was received in the most enthusiastic manner. At Mobile he was hailed as "the champion of the defenceless and suffering inhabitants of Florida," and tendered the freedom of the city.

He was solicited to partake of public dinners both at Mobile and New Orleans, but his services being required upon the western frontier, he declined these honours.

I must now refer the reader to the preparations which have in the mean time been made by Maj. Gen. Scott, who was appointed on the 21st January 1836, to prosecute the war in Florida.

The great disadvantages under which Gen. Scott laboured on taking the command in Florida, necessarily delayed his movements until a very late period. He found the Quartermaster's department extremely deficient, and therefore encountered much difficulty in transporting his supplies to Fort Drane. Ordnance stores were very limited, and much of them unfit for the public service. To penetrate a country like that of Florida, necessarily requires much preparation and great labour; there being no chain of posts or settlements through it, the army are compelled to carry an enormous load with them, and one who has ever been in the service knows the tardiness with which an army moves when encumbered with a heavy baggage train. To increase the evil, large quantities of rain fell about the first of March, and subsequently, which made the roads almost impassable for heavy teams, and broke down the horses very much. Amidst all these difficulties, however, General Scott matured his plan of operations, and on the 13th of March he arrived at Fort Drane with a few companies, preparatory to his taking the field.

Supposing the enemy to be still concentrated at our near the forks of the Ouithlacoochee river, in the neighbourhood of Generals Clinch and Gaines' battle grounds, General Scott adopted the following plan of operations:—

The army assembled in Florida, to constitute three divisions—to be denominated the *Centre, the Right* and *Left Wings.*

The Centre Wing—Composed of a regiment of Alabama volunteers, three companies from Louisiana, and two companies of U. S. Artillery, amounting to about twelve hundred and fifty men, to be commanded by Colonel Wm. Lindsay: to move from Fort Brooke and take a position at or near Chicuchatty, on the 25th of March. Signal guns to be fired each day thereafter, at nine o'clock, A. M., to announce his position.

The Right Wing—Composed of a battalion of Augusta volunteers under acting Major Robertson, a battalion of Georgia volunteers under Major Cooper, Major [John] Douglass' Georgia Cavalry, eleven companies Louisiana volunteers (of Gen. Gaines',) under Col. P. F. Smith, Florida Rangers under Major M'Lemore, the Regulars under Col. Bankhead[123] and Capt. Wharton's[124] company of dragoons, amounting to upwards of two thousand men, to be commanded by Brigadier General Duncan L. Clinch—to move from Fort Drane, and be in position near Camp Izard on the Ouithlacoochee river, between the 26th and 28th of March. Signal guns to be fired at 11 o'clock, A. M.

The Left Wing.—Composed of the South Carolina volunteers under Col. [Abbot] Brisbane, mounted volunteers under Colonels [R. H.] Goodwyn and [P. M.] Butler, and four companies first artillery under Major Kirby—amounting to about fourteen hundred men, to be commanded by Brigadier General Abraham Eustis; to move from Volusia and take a position at or near Pilaklakaha, on the 27th of March. Signal guns to be fired at ten o'clock, A. M. of each day.

Each wing to be composed of three columns; a centre protected by a strong van and rear guard—a right and a left. The baggage train to be placed in the rear of the main column. The *centre* and *left wings,* on assuming their respective positions, will fire signal guns which will be responded to by the *right wing*; the right wing will then move up the cove or great swamp of the Ouithlacoochee in a south-east direction, and drive the Indians south, while the centre will advance to the north, and the left to the west: by which united movement the Indians will be surrounded and left no means of escape.

The operations of the army will be supported by the naval forces under Commodore Dallas, protecting the western coast of the peninsula, to cut off retreat and supplies.

I shall now refer to the respective movements of each wing from the period of their formation at Fort Brooke, Fort King and Volusia, until they arrive in their respective positions at Chicuchatty, Ouithlacoochee and Pilaklakaha.

Colonel Wm. Lindsay arrived at Fort Brooke with eight companies of Alabama volunteers on the 6th of March, where he found a battalion of Floridians under Major Read, and on the 10th was joined by one company of Louisiana volunteers headed by Capt. H. S. Marks, which, with the few United States troops at that post, constituted his command. On the 12th he discovered large fires to the south-east, and it was soon after reported to him that a considerable body of Indians were encamped a few miles distant, when he directed Major

Leigh Read with his battalion to scour the country in that direction. The Major made a forced march during the night, and at day-light the following morning he rushed upon the enemy in their camp and put them to flight with the loss of three killed and six taken prisoners—having also taken from them a considerable quantity of their camp equipage, a few ponies and some cattle.

The whole force of the centre wing being concentrated, and not hearing from Head Quarters, Col. Lindsay determined to proceed as far as the Hillsboro' river, and there erect a stockade with a view to place his supplies nearer to the scene of operations. Having effected this object on the 20th, and named it Fort Alabama, he left Major Read with his battalion in charge of it, and returned to Fort Brooke on the 21st. During his absence from this latter post, despatches were received from General Scott announcing the plan of campaign, and requesting Col. Lindsay to be in position at Chicuchatty on the 25th March. The line of march was accordingly taken up on the 22d, when Major Read and his battalion were relieved by Capt. Marks with the Louisianians and those who were unable to march, and he joined the column. During the 24th and 25th, the rear guard and flankers were annoyed whenever they passed a spot favourable to the operations of the enemy, and on the 26th while passing a dense hammock one man was killed and another wounded. A *charge* being directed by Col. Lindsday, it was very promptly executed by Capt's [Peter] Benham and [James] Blount's companies of Alabama volunteers, which drove the Indians from their covert into an open pine woods, where they showed themselves at a distance of three or four hundred yards, yelling and dancing. After the wing halted and encamped for the night, the enemy again fired on small parties who went to a near pond for water, but one round of canister shot dispersed them. On the 27th one of the Alabamians was killed, and two wounded by the enemy, who was lying in ambuscade; and at noon, whilst halted, the rear guard was fired on, but a brisk return of the fire drove the enemy off.

On the 28th March, three days after the time prescribed in the instructions, they were in position at Camp Broadnax, near Chicuchatty, in pursuance of the orders of General Scott. The country over which they passed was very hilly, and in some places the woods exceedingly dense, which retarded the movements of the wing very much; but the late period at which Colonel Lindsay received the despatches from the Commanding General would have prevented his arriving in position at the time specified, even if the road had been previously cut. No censure is attributable to General Scott, inasmuch as he was unable to mature his plans earlier, in consequence of the limited means of transportation; the great distance which the Indian runner had to accomplish before he reached Colonel Lindsay's post, was also a great obstacle to the accomplishment of his designs. Thus it has been, that a combination of circumstances have interfered with and thwarted the plans of General Scott, to which, perhaps, I shall hereafter allude in detail. Having traced the movements of Colonel Lindsay with the centre wing to his position, where, at the appointed time, a signal gun was fired, I shall now transfer the reader's attention to the movements of the left wing under General Eustis, from the time it leaves Volusia until it reaches Pilaklakaha.

General Eustis arrived at St. Augustine on the 15th of February, when he immediately established a chain of posts at intervals from ten to twenty miles, extending along the Atlantic coast as far south as Musquito [*sic*] Inlet, (*see map,*) in order to drive off the bands of depredators and protect the plantations in that neighbourhood. Colonel Goodwyn's mounted volunteers from South Carolina, having arrived on the 9th of March, the several detachments of the left wing, with the exception of Colonel Butler's battalion and two companies artillery under Major Kirby, were put in motion for Volusia, where they arrived on the 21st, after encountering great obstructions upon the route, having been obliged to cut the road the whole distance. On the 22d the wing commenced crossing the river St. Johns, and when the van guard, consisting of two companies volunteers under Captains [I. A.] Ashby and [Thomas] Fripps, had reached the other side, forty or fifty Indians attacked them from a near hammock with great spirit. Being reinforced by Captain [George] Henry and [Thomas] Hibler's companies, a charge was made upon the enemy, when they fled. Two companies of mounted men were crossed above and below the attacking point in order to cut off retreat, but they scoured the hammocks in vain. Several of the men who entered the hammock at different points were fired upon by others, who supposed them to be the enemy, and wounded two. The loss in the battle with the Indians was three killed and nine wounded. One Indian was found, whom they supposed to be *Euchee Billy*,[125] and it was ascertained that four

Indian bodies had been thrown into the river. On the 24th Lieut. [William] Arnold, with twenty-seven mounted men, was despatched with guides in quest of Colonel Butler and his command, who had not yet joined the wing, having proceeded towards New Smyrna; as the detachment was passing through open pine barren woods, they fell in with a party of twelve or fifteen Indians, who gave battle; the command killed two of the Indians, when the rest effected their escape. General Eustis reflects with much severity upon the conduct of the Lieutenant in command, who, in consequence of his horse being shot, gave orders to retreat, when he might have killed the whole party of the enemy.

The whole force of the left wing being concentrated on the 26th, on the west side of the St. John's river, opposite to Volusia, orders were issued for the distribution of thirteen days' rations to each man, and the line of march to be taken up on the 25th for Pilaklakaha, leaving the sick and wounded with two companies of Colonel Brisbane's regiment, at Volusia, under the command of Major William Gates,[126] U. S. A. From the peculiar character of the country over which they passed on the 26th and 27th,* they made but seven miles in the two days. As they advanced, however, their movements became more rapid, having marched on the 28th thirteen miles. On the 29th the wing reached the Oclawaha, and was obliged to form a bridge, which delayed them until dark, when, having crossed the river, they discovered two fires on the margin of Lake Eustis, which were supposed to be signals from one party of

---

* This day, (the 27th,) General Scott expected the left wing to be in position at Pilaklakaha, about sixty miles from where they were! This speaks volumes for the difficulties against which General Scott had to contend.

Indians to another. Colonel Butler with a small command, accompanied by the gallant General Joseph Shelton, who was serving as a private volunteer, moved towards the spot, and when about four miles distant, four Indians were discovered, who immediately retreated, pursued by the van guard at the head of which was General Shelton, who shot at one of the party when within twenty-five yards, and wounded him in the neck; he then drew a pistol with a deadly aim upon the Indians, but it snapped; and by this time the savage, who had been brought to the knees by the first shot, was enabled to raise his rifle, and shot the General in the hip, the ball passing obliquely through above the bone, and lodged near his back bone, whence it was extracted. Before the Indian had time to reload, one of the volunteers, a Mr. Gibson, galloped rapidly up and discharged the contents of his musket in the back of the Indian, who was then recognized as Yaha Hajo, the second principal war chief, and a man of much influence.

On the 30th, Colonel Goodwyn with his command of mounted men was sent forward to reconnoitre, and when within a few miles of Pilaklakaha, they were attacked while passing a hammock by a considerable number of the enemy—three men were wounded and a few horses shot. General Eustis immediately pushed on to their support with a few volunteers and regulars, and gave orders to scour the hammock, whence the enemy were driven to some distance, when they took to a swamp which was inaccessible to the troops, and they were accordingly recalled. The battle lasted nearly an hour, and the loss on the part of the command was but one man killed. On the 31st March, four days after the time, the left wing arrived at Pilaklakaha and encamped within a short distance of it, having burnt the houses and fences: an express of three men was immediately despatched to Fort King for information of General Scott, and to obtain forage for the horses. At the hour appointed, on the following morning after their arrival, a signal gun was fired, but was unanswered.

The right wing having assembled at Fort Drane, General Scott issued orders to Brigadier General Clinch to put the division in motion on the 25th of March, to take position on the Ouithlacoochee, but a very heavy rain falling on that day the movement was postponed until the 26th, at nine o'clock, A. M. On the 24th, General Clinch despatched two of his negroes in charge of two flat boats, which had been prepared under his own eye, placed on wagon frames, drawn by oxen, and directed them to await the arrival of the wing near the river. The order being given, Major Douglass with his mounted Georgians led off, when each command respectively fell into the line. The order of march was in three columns. The centre, with the baggage train headed by General Clinch; the right, consisting of the Louisiana volunteers under Colonel P. F. Smith, joined in the line at Camp Smith; and the left, commanded by Colonel Bankhead, joined by Lieutenant Colonel Foster's battalion of U. S. troops at Camp Twiggs—General Scott and staff, with an escort of dragoons, taking position in the centre. The indefatigable Colonel Gadsden was appointed Quartermaster General[*] for Florida, and Acting Inspector General.

---

[*] It is to be hoped that the reader will not confound the duties of Col. Gadsden with those of the Quartermaster General *at Washington* and his

The first encampment of the wing was about nine miles from Fort Drane, when news was brought to us at the fort by two of the Macon volunteers, that themselves and several others who were left with a broken down team some distance in the rear, and out of sight of the column, had been attacked by Indians, and one man killed. Captain Lendrum immediately sent a small detachment of mounted men to ascertain the facts, but they returned without discovering any traces of wagon, man or Indians. It was afterwards ascertained, that others had escaped to the column, when a detachment of cavalry was despatched to the spot, and discovered a black man dead and the cart broken into pieces. Late on the 28th, the wing arrived near the Ouithlacoochee, and encamped about two hundred and fifty yards from Camp Izard. At four o'clock the following morning, the river bank was occupied by sharp shooters and two pieces of artillery, to cover the crossing, which had been selected very judiciously by Col. Gadsden. Mr. Floster Blodget, of Augusta, belonging to Capt. Robertson's Richmond Blues, most gallantly proffered to swim the river and attach a rope to a tree upon the opposite side, to facilitate the passage of the wing. Every moment his friends expected to see him fall a victim to his noble daring, but he reached it in safety and planted the flag of the company upon the bank— while the record of his chivalry is preserved in history by the well-merited tribute of General Scott, in naming the crossing place "Blodget's Ferry." As soon as this feat was accom-

---

dependants; as Col. Gadsden's appointment was as an *attaché* to the staff of Gen. Scott, and during the operations of the army *his* duties were most admirably performed.

plished, the two flat boats prepared at Fort Drane were launched, and a detachment of two companies of artillery crossed, under command of Major Zantzinger, followed by Colonel Smith's regiment of Louisiana volunteers, and the fourth infantry, when the whole train was enabled to pass during the day. The Washington Cavalry, Capt. Malone, and the Hancock troop, Capt. [John] Swinney, discovered a ford about one and a half miles lower down the river, at which they passed and joined the wing at Camp Blodget. As the rear division of the column was crossing, after the train had been passed, the Indians attacked them, but were quickly repulsed by two discharges from the six-pounders, and a volley from the rear guard under the gallant Major Belton. A few shots were fired into the camp during the night, but no damage sustained. On the morning of the 30th, at 11 o'clock, having reached a small prairie island, surrounded by hammock, upon a chain of lakes* running near and parallel with the river, they discovered a number of the enemy partly concealed by the grass; the baggage train was drawn up and placed under a guard of three hundred men, when the troops were formed for an attack, but the Indians holding up their hands and manifesting a disposition to surrender, Adjutant Barrow of the Louisiana volunteers, accompanied by *Nero* an interpreter, and an Indian sub-chief, *Billy,* went forward to meet them. Their movements being somewhat suspicious, the Adjutant returned to the column, when a *charge* was ordered, and the enemy were completely routed, leaving part of their breakfast

---

* This chain of lakes is called Oloklikaha, (spotted lake,) being dotted with islands of from a quarter of a mile to one mile in length, which are principally covered with dense cypress swamps and hammocks; some of them, however, have been under cultivation.

uncooked. They were pursued by the brave Louisianaians under Colonel Smith, the Georgians under Major Robertson, and the infantry under Colonel Foster, for a distance of four miles, both pursuers and pursued keeping up a continuous running fire, when, as it was growing late, the detachment encamped. Resuming the line early the next morning, the 31st, the enemy were again discovered on another island, when a disposition was made of the right column under Colonel Smith, and the left under Colonel Bankhead to attack upon two opposite points. The approach to both was extremely difficult, and inaccessible to any but infantry troops, and it was not without great effort that the men struggled through it. When the right division reached the firm ground, they were met by a very sharp and spirited discharge from the enemy's rifles, but, gallantly dashing forward, the enemy was dislodged from his position and pursued for three or four miles, when, having crossed the river, pursuit was given up. Colonel Smith and the volunteers conducted with great spirit and courage throughout; as also did the others. The left division was also opposed at the opposite point when within one hundred yards of the hammock by a heavy fire from the enemy, but a few discharges from the six-pounder, which had been forced to the edge of the morass, silenced them and enabled the troops to reach the hammock, whence the enemy were soon compelled to fly, and the pursuit continued for two miles under a heavy running fire from them. Finding it impossible to penetrate the dense cypress swamp and cross the river, the two divisions met and returned to the baggage train, which, as before stated, had been left several miles in the rear, where they encamped. The loss during these two days was four killed and nine wounded—three of the former and four of the latter being Louisianians.

The following morning, the 1st of April, the entire wing proceeded along the lakes, and having reached the southeastern termination of them without being able to find the enemy, General Scott directed a post of observation to be established, and left Major Cooper with his battalion, amounting to about three hundred and fifty men and one company of artillery, a field-piece and seventeen days' provisions. The next morning, the wing continued its march to Tampa Bay, (proper,) where it arrived without other incidents occurring, on the 5th of April, after a fatiguing march—being obliged to cut the road the whole distance. On their arrival here they found that the centre wing under Col. Lindsay, had preceded them one day, being obliged to return for provisions.

The reader will remember that the *centre* wing, under Colonel Lindsay, took position at Camp Broadnax near Chicuchatty, on the 28th of March. Here the enemy fired on the horses and guard attending them, when a detachment of four companies, under Major Leigh Read, charged upon and drove them off without any loss to his troops. On the 30th two parties of mounted men under Captains Taylor and Roulett were sent out in search of cattle, and they succeeded in capturing enough to supply the wing for four days, although the supplies of bread and salt were exhausted. The friendly Indians also succeeded in killing a hostile sub-chief by the name of Charley Fixico. During the night the sentinels were frequently fired upon, but without sustaining any injury. An unsuccessful attempt was made during the 31st to procure additional supplies, as provisions were very limited, and having barely sufficient meat, without bread or salt, to last them to Fort Brooke; and as no response to his signals had been made by the other wings within his hearing, and not knowing their respective positions, he supposed that the objects contemplated by the plan of campaign had been frustrated, and orders were therefore issued by the Colonel to return to Fort Brooke, where the wing arrived during the night of the fourth of April, having been absent fourteen days on ten days' provisions.

On his arrival at Fort Alabama near the Hillsboro' river. Colonel Lindsay was informed, that that post was attacked about eight o'clock on the morning of the 27th of March, by an Indian force supposed to be three or four hundred strong, who surrounded the breastwork and fought with most determined fury for two hours and a half, when they were repulsed with a loss of about fifteen men. The enemy continued to hang around the work both day and night, until the approach of the centre wing, when they fled. The loss on the part of the garrison was one man, killed and scalped outside the work, and two wounded. Colonel Lindsay ordered the command to continue there to protect the post.

General Eustis with the left wing, being in the same predicament as Colonel Lindsay with the centre, and hearing no response to his signal, took up the line of march on the 2d of April, leaving his position near Pilaklakaha, and struck the military road a little north of Dade's battle ground, for Fort Brooke. On the third the *left* fell upon the trail of the *centre*, when General Eustis sent an express to Colonel Lindsay, which was replied to on the 4th, and, continuing his route towards Fort Brooke, was met by orders from General Scott to encamp on the military road, about sixteen miles from that post. On the 5th General Eustis and his staff proceeded to Fort Brooke to report in person to General Scott.

The three divisions of the army having now arrived at or in the vicinity of Fort Brooke, after marching through the enemy's country without meeting him in any considerable force, it became necessary to ascertain, as near as possible, their new location preparatory to the opening of another campaign. Taking all the circumstances in connexion, they would naturally justify the belief that, having penetrated the *cove* sufficiently to discover whether there was any trace of a large settlement, and finding but very small parties—that they had removed their families and plunder to a more secure and inaccessible retreat. But this question is likely to puzzle us; Could they find a more secure harbour for them than where they now are, since it has eluded the vigilance and scrutiny of our army, although it appears that they passed within a short distance of the habitation? The opinion, however, that they had gone to the south of the peninsula, and taken up their abode in the everglades, was much strengthened by the report of a mixed Indian who had been connected with a gang of desperadoes in the neighbourhood of Charlotte Harbour, and was captured by Lieutenant Powell[127] and a few Spaniards. He stated that the Indians were concentrated in the neighbourhood of Pease Creek [Peace River], and had large supplies of ammunition at Charlotte Harbour, which determined General Scott to accept the services of Colonel Smith and the Louisiana forces to proceed by water to Charlotte Harbour, and move north, while the South Carolina mounted men, under Colonel Goodwyn, was ordered to march to the lake at the head of Pease's Creek for the purpose of driving them down. Having burnt a large Indian village on the left bank of that stream, and finding no signs of Indians in that quarter, the command returned to the Hillsborough river, and joined the left wing.—The Louisiana troops left Fort Brooke on the 10th of April, and landed at Pease's creek on the 17th; they immediately pressed forward, but the weather was so excessively oppressive, and the men being worn down and exhausted by their previous marches— many that were destitute of clothing with scarce a shoe upon their feet or a shirt upon their back—were obliged to return to the camp. Out of more than seven hundred Louisianians who volunteered in January, and entered the field early in February, but one hundred and thirty were now left who were able to endure the fatigues of another march. With these, however, and a small party of marines from the United States vessels in that vicinity, Col. Smith determined to proceed and accomplish the objects prescribed in the letter of instructions to him. He accordingly embarked with one-half of his command in a few canoes, whilst the others journeyed by land in search of a convenient encamping ground. On the 19th the troops came to a small Indian camp, which had been deserted but a few hours previous, where they discovered numerous articles which had doubtless been pillaged from the settlements on the lower part of the peninsula; here they halted for the night. They re-embarked again on the 20th, but were unable to proceed far before the obstructions in the river compelled them to return and march by land. After an absence of three days, without discovering the enemy, and being without provisions, Colonel Smith deemed it prudent to return to his transports, and thence to Fort Brooke, which post he reached on the 27th April, when the troops were ordered to return to New Orleans and there be mustered out of service. Col. Smith in the meantime proceeded to St. Marks pursuant to instructions, to report in person to General Scott.

The right wing having remained at Tampa Bay from the 5th until the 13th of April, General Scott issued orders to Gen. Clinch to proceed towards Fort Drane, and, after relieving Maj. Cooper, to co-operate as far as practicable with the centre wing, under Col. Lindsay, who left Fort Brooke on the same day for the purpose of penetrating the cove in a different direction from that pursued by the *right* on its march to Tampa, and scouring the forks of the Ouithlacoochee. Whilst Col. Lindsay was engaged in constructing a defence for his baggage train on the military road near to the Big Ouithlacoochee, Gen. Clinch encamped within four miles of Fort Cooper, and despatched the Washington and Jefferson Cavalry with a few wagons, under Captain Malone, to relieve the garrison, with instructions that, should he meet the enemy, to advise General Clinch immediately. When about three miles distant from the main body, a vigorous fire was poured into the ranks by a considerable number of Indians in ambush, who retreated before Capt. Malone was enabled to return the fire. Upon being reinforced by the fourth infantry under Col. Bankhead, the hammock was throughly [*sic*] scoured, without discovering the enemy or whence they had fled. Two men of the Washington Troop were badly wounded. The detachment then pursued its course

without further interruption, and arrived at Fort Cooper much
to the joy and satisfaction of its inmates, who were entirely
destitute of provisions in consequence of the Indians having
intercepted the few beeves which were left by Gen. Clinch,
and driven them off.

Major Cooper stated, that whilst occupied in strengthening
his defences, on the fourth day after the right wing left him,
the Indians made a desperate attack upon him with a force of
several hundred men, determined to carry the work by storm.
But he made a sortie, and advanced within a few yards of them
through a very heavy fire before he succeeded in routing them.
They retreated, however, in spite of the efforts of their chiefs
to make them stand. For thirteen successive days the garrison
was annoyed in this manner, and, upon every occasion, a sortie was made, when, after an hour or two hard fighting, they
were repulsed. The loss of the battalion during this period was
one man killed and about twenty wounded. Major Cooper and
his battalion soon joined the wing under Clinch, when they
retraced their steps about two miles, and struck upon a trail
which was followed two days without seeing the enemy. The
signal gun of Col. Lindsay was then heard, when Gen. Clinch
pushed forward to form a junction with him, and that evening
found the centre wing encamped upon the Big Ouithlacoochee. Col. Lindsay and several of his men had been confined by sickness since he commenced the march, and, whilst
crossing the Hillsboro' river, he was fired upon by the Indians,
who killed Mr. James Branham of the Alabama volunteers,
and then retreated. Not having found the enemy in any numbers, the two wings separated—the *centre* returning to its baggage train, and thence to Fort Brooke—and the *right* proceed-
ing by the military road to Fort King, where they arrived on
the 25th of April, having been fired upon in the neighbourhood of Fort King, and Mr. Bostwick of the Jefferson Troop,
wounded. They also fell in with about two hundred head of
cattle and several ponies.

After the junction of Col. Goodwyn's mounted regiment, the left wing, accompanied by Gen. Scott, took up the line of march on the 18th, via Big Ouithlacoochee and Pilaklakaha, for Volusia. On the night of the 22d, a small party of the enemy fired on the camp, and wounded one man and two horses. On the 24th, another small party was met, and pursuit made, but, secreting themselves in a hammock, they eluded detection. The wing with Gen. Eustis arrived at Volusia on evening of the 25th, and on the 28th all the volunteers from Carolina proceeded to St. Augustine, and were there discharged.

On his arrival at Fort Brooke, Colonel Lindsay was directed by the Commanding General to relieve the garrison at Fort Alabama, and disband the volunteers, leaving the regulars at the former post. The Alabama regiment and two companies of U. S. troops were detached for this purpose under command of Col. Childers. Having evacuated the post and left a considerable quantity of powder in the magizine [*sic*], in such manner as to ignite upon forcing the door, the command had only reached the distance of two miles when an explosion took place, and it is supposed, from an attempt made by the Indians to open the vault. Pursuing their course, the division arrived at Clonoto Lassa [Thonotosassa] Creek, near Camp Shelton, on the 27th of April, and while passing a hammock, a heavy and destructive fire was opened upon them by a large body of the unseen enemy; a spirited engagement ensued, but as soon as the troops passed into the covert the enemy gave way and made a rapid retreat, having killed four and wounded nineteen of the Alabamians. On the arrival of the detachment at Fort Brooke, they were discharged, and embarked for their respective destinations.

Gen. Scott, accompanied by Col. Gadsden, Capt. Canfield, and Lieut. Johnson, with a detachment of seventeen men, embarked in the steamboat Essayons at Volusia, for the purpose of penetrating by the St. Johns the south part of the peninsula, as far as practicable, and selecting a site nearer to the seat of war, as a depot for provisions, &c. He proceeded to the head of Lake Monroe, but the boat was unable to pass over the bar, and he was therefore compelled to return, after having established a depot a few miles below Lake Monroe—(*See map.*)

Gen. Scott then proceeded to take charge of the campaign against the Creeks.

A small command of Floridians, which had been left by Major M'Lemore on the 5th of April in a blockhouse on the Ouithlacoochee, about fifteen miles above its mouth, were, by a strange oversight, entirely neglected, and they were assailed on the 12th of April, by a very large body of Indians, who attempted to burn the house by shooting fire-arrows into the roof. On the 15th they were surrounded by nearly one thousand of the enemy, but they succeeded in repulsing them. Having remained in this situation, constantly annoyed by the Indians for a period of fifty days, with nothing to subsist on but corn and water, they were relieved by Maj. Leigh Read, who ascended the river with a small detachment and brought them off without firing a shot.

Books Published by the Seminole Wars Foundation

The Origin, Progress and Conclusion of the Florida War, by Capt. John T. Sprague

Reminiscences of the Second Seminole War, by John Bemrose.

Amidst a Storm of Bullets: The Diary of Lt. Henry Prince in Florida, 1836-1842, Frank Laumer, editor

Fear and Anxiety on the Florida Frontier: Articles on the Second Seminole War, by Joe Knetsch

The Fort King Road: Then and Now, by Jerry C. Morris and Jeffrey A. Hough

This Miserable Pride of a Soldier: The Letters and Journals of Col. William S. Foster in the Second Seminole War, John and Mary Lou Missall, editors

This Torn Land: Poetry of the Second Seminole War, John and Mary Lou Missall, editors

Additional Books by John & Mary Lou Missall

The Seminole Wars: America's Longest Indian Conflict (University Press of Florida)

Hollow Victory: A Novel of the Second Seminole War (Florida Historical Society Press)

Available from our website: www.seminolewars.us

Notes

Note: Unless otherwise noted, names of the Volunteers were taken from "Index to Compiled Service Records of Volunteer Soldiers Who Served During Indian Wars and Disturbances, 1815-1858," National Archives Microfilm Publication M629, 42 rolls; Records of the Adjutant General's Office, 1780s-1912, RG 94, National Archives, Washington, D.C.

[1] Francis B. Heitman, *Historical Register and Dictionary of the United States Army, 1789-1903* (Washington, D. C.: Government Printing Office, 1903), 802. Gen. Gaines to Sec. of War Joel Poinsett, 15 April 1837, recommending Woodburne Potter for a lieutenant commission in the infantry. Correspondence: General-English Documents (Houston Endowment Texana Collection, MS MC042, San Jacinto Museum of History, Abert & Ethel Herzstein Library). Page 11, *Index to the Executive Documents and Reports of Commanders of the House of Representatives*. 22-25 Congress, Dec. 1831-March 1839.

[2] Heitman, 802. Army & Navy Chronicle, 305, 309, 312, 329; U.S. Returns from Military Posts, 1806-1916, January-December 1838 (Fort Gibson and Jefferson Barracks) and March 1839 (Fort Brooke).

[3] *The Philadelphia Navy Yard: from the Birth of the US Navy to the Nuclear Age*, by Jeffery M. Dorwart with Jean K. Wolf, 2001, The Barra Foundation, Univ. of Penn. Press, 76. Historic Pennsylvania Church and Town Records, 1708-1985, Reel 98.

[4] Camp Izard, a temporary fortification built near the Withlacoochee River and named after 1st Lt. James Farley Izard, who was mortally wounded on 28 February 1836 during the attack on Gen. Edmund Gaines's command. The site is currently managed by the Southwest Florida Water Management District; Lt. Henry Prince, *Amidst a Storm of Bullets: The Diary of Lt. Henry Prince in Florida, 1836-1842*, ed. Frank Laumer (Tampa: University of Tampa Press, 1998), 16-18, 23-24, 149n50; George McCall, *Letters from the Frontiers* (Philadelphia, 1868), 326.

[5] Bvt. Maj. Francis Langhorne Dade, 4th Inf., in command of 107 officers and men, was killed by Seminoles 28 December 1835 on their march to Fort King, FL Territory, with only two soldiers surviving; Frank Laumer, *Dade's Last Command* (Gainesville: University Press of Florida, 1995), 41-45, 182; Sprague, 90, Prince, 5-6, 12-13, 147n7; Heitman, 350.

[6] Gen. Wiley Thompson, Seminole Indian Agent at the commencement of the Second Seminole War. Former Georgia Militia officer (1817-1824), Georgia Senator (1817-1819), and United States Congressman (1821-1833). Killed by Osceola and others on 28 December 1835 at Fort King; *Biographical Directory of the United States Congress, 1774-Present*, http://bioguide.congress.gov/scripts/biodisplay.pl?index=T000222.

[7] Lewis Cass, Governor of Michigan Territory (1813-1831), Secretary of War (1831-1836), Ambassador to France (1836-1842), U.S. Senator from Michigan (1845-1857), U.S. Secretary of State (1857-1860); *Biographical Directory,* http://bioguide.congress.gov/scripts/biodisplay.pl?index=C000233.

[8] Brig. Gen. Winfield Scott, Brig. Gen. (1814), bvt. Maj. Gen. (1814) for gallantry at Chippewa and Niagara, Maj. Gen. (1841), Commander in Chief of the Army (1841-1846), bvt. Lt. Gen. (1847) for eminent service in Mexican War in capturing Veracruz and battle of San Juan de Ulloa; Heitman, 870.

[9] Maj. Gen. Thomas Sidney Jesup, bvt. Lt. Col. and Col. (1814) for gallantry in battles of Chippewa and Niagara, Lt. Col., 3rd Arty. (1817-1818), Col. Adj. Gen. and Brig. Gen. QM Gen. (1818), Maj. Gen. (1828) for ten years faithful service in one grade; Heitman, 573.

[10] Major Generals Edmund P. Gaines and Winfield Scott were the second and third highest ranking officers in the army and were engaged in a long-running dispute over who was the senior officer. The dispute centered on brevet rank, a device used by Congress that promoted officers but did not give them a corresponding pay raise. Some officers (Gaines) did not feel it counted toward seniority, while others (Scott) felt it did; John K. Mahon, *History of the Second Seminole War, 1835-1842,* Rev. ed. (Gainesville: University of Florida Press, 1992), 138-139.

[11] Col. Joseph M. White, Florida Territorial Delegate to U. S. Congress (1825-1837), *Biographical Directory,* http://bioguide.congress.gov/scripts/biodisplay.pl?index=W000383.

[12] Bvt. Brig. Gen. Duncan Lamont Clinch, in command of troops in Florida Territory (1827-1836), resigned Sept. 1836; Heitman, 310; Mahon, 65-66.

[13] Capt. Gustavus S. (Augustus) Drane, supervised construction of fortification that was given his name; Mahon, 107; Prince, 9, 148n21; Heitman, 382.

[14] Fort Drane, a picket work about 20 miles northwest of Fort King on Gen. Clinch's sugar plantation "Auld Lang Syne;" John T. Sprague, *The Origin, Progress and Conclusion of the Florida War,* a Reproduction of the 1848 Edition (Tampa: University of Tampa Press, 2000), 118; Mahon, 103, 107.

[15] This is in reference to General Andrew Jackson's 1818 campaign into Spanish Florida in what became known as the First Seminole War; Mahon, 25-27.

[16] Micanopy (Sint Chakkee), Head chief of the Seminoles at the war's commencement; Mahon, 125-127.

[17] Pilaklakaha (Peliklikaha, Peliklakaha, Palaklikaha), aka Abraham's Old Town, village of Black Seminole leader Abraham; Mahon, 143.

[18] Jumper (Ote Emathla, Otee-Emathlar), influential Seminole leader, Chief Micanopy's brother-in-law; Sprague, 97; Mahon, 127.

188

[19] Wahoo Swamp, a favorite Indian haunt, on the west side of the Withla-coochee River from the Cove; location of Battle of Wahoo Swamp (21 Nov. 1836) during Gov. Richard Call's campaign; Sprague, 163-166, 271; Mahon, 105, 184-186.

[20] Abraham, slave, interpreter, and advisor to Chief Micanopy; Mahon, 62, 128.

[21] Holata Mico (Blue King), Pease Creek Tallahassee band, refused emi-gration; Mahon, 62, 95-96.

[22] Yaha Hajo (Yahadjo, Yahahadjo), Seminole leader named in the Treaty of Payne's Landing and Treaty of Fort Gibson; Sprague, 75, 78; Mahon, 79, 157.

[23] Arpiucki (Abiaca, Sam Jones), influential Mikasuki leader and medicine man; Sprague, 99, 318-319 Mahon, 127-128.

[24] Assiola (Osceola, Asi-Yoholo, Tallahassee Tustenuggee, Powell), mem-ber of the Red Stick branch of Creek Indians, influential leader during the Second Seminole War who most represented the war spirit and symbol of Indian resistance to emigration, captured under flag of truce (1837), im-prisoned in Fort Marion at St. Augustine then transferred to Fort Moultrie, Charleston, SC where he died; Sprague, 99-100, 216; Mahon, 91-92.

[25] Coa Hajo (Coa Hadjo), influential Seminole leader, against immigration; Sprague, 217; Mahon, 96.

[26] Treaty of Moultrie Creek (1823), established a reservation for the Indi-ans in the central portion of the Florida Territory; Sprague, 20-24.

[27] William Pope DuVal, Governor of Florida Territory (1822-1834); *Bio-graphical Directory,*
http://bioguide.congress.gov/scripts/biodisplay.pl?index=D000577.

[28] John Blunt, Seminole leader; Sprague, 22-24.

[29] Bernardo (Bernard) Segui, commissioner to negotiate Treaty of Fort Moultrie (1823); Sprague, 20; Mahon, 40.

[30] Col. Gad Humphreys, Seminole agent (1822-1830); Sprague, 19-70.

[31] Horatio S. Dexter, earlier settler, negotiator for the Seminoles, witnessed the Treaty of Fort Moultrie; Sprague, 22; Mahon, 42-43.

[32] Col. James Gadsden, commissioner to negotiate Treaty of Fort Moultrie; Sprague, 20-24.

[33] Treaty of Payne's Landing (1832), called for relinquishment of Indian claims to land in the Florida Territory in exchange for land west of the Mississippi; Sprague, 74-78.

[34] Cudjoe (Cudjo), Black interpreter; Mahon, 78.

[35] Maj. John Phagan, Seminole agent (1830-1834); Sprague, 72, 79.

[36] Treaty of Fort Gibson (1833), supposedly established Seminole satisfac-tion with land west of the Mississippi and agreement to emigrate; Sprague, 76-78.

[37] John Henry Eaton, Secretary of War (1829-1831) and Governor of Florida Territory (1834-1836); *Biographical Directory,* http://bioguide.congress.gov/scripts/biodisplay.pl?index=E000024.
[38] James Monroe, fifth President of the United States (1817-1825); *Biographical Directory,* http://bioguide.congress.gov/scripts/biodisplay.pl?index=M000858.
[39] Benjamin Franklin Butler, Attorney General (1833-1838), acting Secretary of War (1836-1837); Sprague, 83; Mahon, 183.
[40] Richard K. Call, West Florida militia general (1823), Governor of Florida Territory (1835-1840, 1841-1844); *Biographical Directory,* http://bioguide.congress.gov/scripts/biodisplay.pl?index=C000050.
[41] Mr. William Everett (Everitt), filed affidavit in Tallahassee (1828) for claims to certain slaves among the Seminoles; Sprague, 59.
[42] Fort King, Indian Agency, built in 1827, future City of Ocala; Sprague, 21; Mahon, 88.
[43] Capt. John B. F. Russell, graduated Military Academy at West Point [hereafter MA] (1818), Capt., 5th Inf. (1830); Heitman, 853; George W. Cullum, *Biographical Register of the Officers and Graduates of the U. S. Military Academy at West Point, N. Y.,* 3rd ed., Vol. 1 (Boston: Houghton, Mifflin and Co., 1891), 201.
[44] Col. Mathew Arbuckle, Col., 7th Inf. (1820), bvt. Brig. Gen. (1830) for ten years faithful service in one grade, Heitman, 168.
[45] Lt. Joseph Whipple Harris, graduated MA (1825), 1st Lt., 3rd Arty. (1833), disbursing agent for Seminole migration (1833-1837); Sprague, 84; Mahon. 96; Heitman, 503; Cullum, 347.
[46] Pvt. Kinsley H. Dalton, 3rd Arty., killed by Indians while carrying mail from Fort Brooke to Fort King (Aug. 1835); Mahon, 99.
[47] Maj. Francis Smith Belton, commanding officer at Fort Brooke, Maj. Adj. Inspector General (1820-1821) after being reinstated, Capt. 2nd Arty. (1821), Maj. 1st Arty. (July 1838) and 4th Arty. (Sept. 1838), Lt. Col, 3rd Arty. (1845), bvt. Col. (1847) for gallantry in battles of Contreras and Churubusco, Mexico, Col., 4th Arty. (1857); Mahon, 101; Heitman, 209.
[48] Brig. Gen. Joseph M. Hernandez, Florida Territorial Delegate to U. S. Congress (1822-1823), militia general (1835-1838); *Biographical Directory,* http://bioguide.congress.gov/scripts/biodisplay.pl?index=H000533.
[49] Col. John Warren, from Jacksonville, commander of the FL militia, supported regular troops at Battle of Withlacoochee (31 December 1835); Sprague, 230; Mahon, 101, 179; Benjamin Homans, ed. *Army and Navy Chronicle* [hereafter *A&NC*] 5 (21 December 1837), 387; F & S Co., 1 (Warren's) FL Mounted Militia (1836-1837), NARA, M629, Roll 40.
[50] Dr. John McLemore, later Major in the Florida militia; Sprague, 150-153; Mahon, 101; Maj. in McCants' Battalion FL Militia, NARA, M629, Roll 25.

[51] Col. Richard C. Parish, FL Vols., supported regular troops at Battle of Withlacoochee (31 December 1835); Homans, *A&NC* 5 (21 December 1837), 387; Prince, 6; Col. Richard C. Parish 2 Reg't FL Militia (Col. R. C. Parish); NARA, M629, Roll 29.

[52] Col. Leigh Read, Florida militia officer, later Major and Brig. Gen.; Sprague, 136, 150-154, Mahon, 153, 272-273; Brig. Gen. Leigh Read, 1 Brigade FL Militia (1836-1837), Read's Brig. FL Militia, 3 month services (1840, 1840-41, 1841); NARA, M629, Roll 31.

[53] Capt. George Washington Gardiner, graduated MA (1814), bvt. Capt., 2nd Arty. (1828), Capt. (1832), killed at Dade's Battle 28 December 1835; Heitman, 445; Cullum, 111.

[54] Capt. Upton Sinclair Fraser, 3rd Arty. (1828), killed at Dade's Battle 28 December 1835; Laumer, 39-40; Heitman, 434.

[55] Lt. Robert Rich Mudge, graduated MA (1833), 2nd Lt., 3rd Arty. (1835), killed at Dade's Battle 28 December 1835; Laumer, 142-144; Heitman, 734; Cullum, 546-547.

[56] Lt. John Low Keais, graduated MA (1835) and promoted bvt. 2nd Lt., 3rd Arty. (July 1835), killed at Dade's Battle 28 December 1835; Heitman, 586; Cullum, 594-595.

[57] Lt. Richard Henderson, graduated MA (1835), promoted bvt. 2nd Lt., 2nd Arty. (July 1835), killed at Dade's Battle 28 December 1835; Heitman, 522; Cullum, 594.

[58] Dr. John Slade Gatlin, Asst. Surgeon (1834), killed at Dade's Battle 28 December 1835; Heitman, 450.

[59] Lt. William Elon Basinger, graduated MA (1830), promoted bvt. 2nd Lt., 2nd Arty. and 2nd Lt., 2nd Arty. (1830), killed at Dade's Battle 28 December 1835; Laumer, 42-44; Heitman, 197; Cullum, 448.

[60] Pvt. Ransom Clark, 2nd Arty., severely wounded survivor of Dade's Battle; Laumer, 45, 165, 230, his testimony 235-239.

[61] Maj. John Mountfort, 2nd Arty., bvt. Capt. (1814) for gallantry in attack on Plattsburg, NY, bvt. Maj. (1829) for faithful service in one grade; Heitman, 733.

[62] Maj. Gen. Edmund Pendleton Gaines, bvt. Maj. Gen. (1814) for gallantry in defeating the enemy at Fort Erie, in command of the Western Department of the Army; Mahon, 144; Heitman, 442.

[63] Pvt. John Thomas was a member of Dade's command who had injured his back while lifting a cannon from the river before the battle and did not participate. The only two survivors were Pvts. Joseph Sprague and Ransom Clarke. Sprague was wounded in the arm, and Clark suffered multiple wounds, including a flesh wound to his right temple, wounds in the right shoulder and arm above the elbow which deprived him use of that arm, a wound in the right thigh that broke the bone, and in the back, which penetrated the lung; Laumer, 99-100, 106, 212-213, 230-231.

[64] Lt. Walter Scott Chandler, graduated MA (1830) and promoted bvt. 2nd Lt. and 2nd Lt., 2nd Arty., (1830); Heitman, 295; Cullum, 182.

[65] Pvt. Joseph Sprague, 3rd Arty., wounded survivor of Dade's Battle; Laumer, 213, 231]

[66] There is no record of a servant, and the interpreter, a slave named Luis Pacheco, was taken prisoner by the Indians; Laumer, 241-243.

[67] Capt. Thomas W. Lendrum, graduated MA (1815), Capt., 3rd Arty. (1828-1838), Maj. Commissary of Subsistence (1838); Heitman, 628, Cullum, 140-141.

[68] Lt. Francis Littleberry Dancy, graduated MA (1826), 1st Lt., 2nd Arty. (1832), Lt. Col. Fla. Vols. (1840), Col. (1840), Capt. AQM and Col. Adj. Gen. (1861-1865); Heitman, 352; Cullum, 369.

[69] Maj. Alexander C. W. Fanning, graduated MA (1812), bvt. Maj. (1814) for gallantry in defense of Ft. Erie, bvt. Lt. Col. (1824) for ten years faithful service in one grade, Maj., 4th Arty. (1832), bvt. Col. for gallantry at Withlacoochee (1835), Lt. Col, 4th Arty. (1838); Heitman, 412-413; Cullum, 107-109.

[70] Maj. James G. Cooper, FL Vols., supported regular troops at Battle of Withlacoochee (31 December 1835); Homans, *A&NC* 5 (21 December 1837), 387.

[71] Capt. William Montrose Graham, graduated MA (1817), Capt., 4th Inf. (1832), commanding officer at Fort King, bvt. Maj. for gallantry at Withlacoochee (1835), Maj., 2nd Inf. (1847), Lt. Col., 11th Inf. (1847), killed in Battle of Molino del Rey, Mexico; Mahon, 87, Heitman, 468, Cullum, 157.

[72] Lt. Campbell Graham, graduated MA (1822), promoted bvt. 2nd Lt. and 2nd Lt., 3rd Arty. (1822), bvt. Capt. for gallantry at Withlacoochee (1835), bvt. Capt. Asst. Topo. Eng. (1837), Capt. Topo Eng. (1838), Maj. (1857); Heitman, 467; Cullum, 281-282.

[73] Lt. Thomas P. Ridgely (Ridgely), 2nd Lt., 2nd Arty. (1835), 1st Lt. (1836), Capt. (1846); Sprague, 92; Heitman, 830.

[74] Lt. Col. William J. Mills, FL militia, supported regular troops at Battle of Withlacoochee (31 December 1835); Mahon, 257; Sprague, 92; Homans, *A&NC* 5 (21 December 1837), 387; NARA, M629, Roll 26.

[75] Maj. Robert Gamble, FL Vols. He established a sugar plantation along the Manatee River in 1844 under the 1842 Armed Occupation Act. The Gamble Plantation is now a historic state park in Ellenton, FL; Michael C. Schene, "Sugar Along the Manatee: Major Robert Gamble, Jr. and the Development of Gamble Plantation," *Tequesta* 41 (1981): 69-81.

[76] Maj. John S. Lytle, paymaster (1834), acting aide-de-camp to Gen. Clinch; Sprague, 92; Heitman, 651.

[77] Capt. Charles Mellon, Capt., 2nd Arty. (1835), killed in action with Seminole Indians at Lake Monroe (8 Feb. 1837). Camp Monroe renamed Fort Mellon in his honor; Sprague, 170; Mahon, 199; Heitman, 702.

[78] Capt. Lemuel Gates, 1st Arty. (1835), in command at Fort Drane, died (1836); Heitman, 449; Mahon, 173.

[79] Lt. George Henry Talcott, graduated MA (1831), bvt. 1st Lt., 3rd Arty. (1835) for gallantry in Fla. War, 1st Lt. Ord. (1838), Capt. Ord. (1847), Maj. Vols. (1847-48), bvt. Lt. Col. (1847) for gallantry at Battle of Molino del Rey, Mexico; Heitman, 943; Cullum, 474-475.

[80] Lt. Erastus A. Capron, graduated MA (1833), promoted bvt. 2nd Lt., 1st Arty. (1833), 2nd Lt. (1834), 1st Lt. (1836), Capt. (1847), killed at battle of Churubusco, Mexico (1847); Heitman, 281; Cullum, 545.

[81] Lt. John Graham, graduated MA (1834), promoted bvt. 2nd Lt., 4th Inf. (1834), 2nd Lt. (1836), 1st Lt. 2nd Dragoons (1836), Capt. (1837), Adj. Gen. of Territory of Florida (1840-41); Heitman, 468; Cullum, 585-586.

[82] Capt. William S. Maitland, graduated MA (1820), bvt. Capt. for gallantry at Withlacoochee (1835); Heitman, 685; Cullum, 261.

[83] Lt. Alexander Scamell Brooks, bvt. Maj. (1814) for gallantry at Battle of Plattsburg, NY, Lt. Col., 4th Arty. (1835), died in steamboat *Dolphin* explosion in St. James Bay, FL (7 Dec. 1836); Heitman, 248; Jacob Rhett Motte, *Journey into Wilderness: An Army Surgeon's Account of Life in Camp and Field during the Creek and Seminole Wars, 1836-1838,* ed. James F. Sunderman (Gainesville: University of Florida Press, 1963), 255n8.

[84] 2nd Lt. John Yeoman (Youman), 4 Reg't. Mtd. (Warren's, 1836) FL Militia; NARA, M629, Roll 42; Homans, *A&NC* 5 (21 December 1837), 387.

[85] Dr. Richard Weightman, post surgeon (1818), assistant surgeon (1821); Heitman, 1014.

[86] Mr. Philip Solano, planter residing on the St. John's River, accused of instigating a fight with the Indians at nearby Cabbage Swamp in 1825; Sprague, 30-33; Mahon, 59.

[87] Maj. Benjamin A. Putnam, lawyer and St. Augustine resident, commanding officer of the Fla. volunteer St. Augustine Guards; Sprague, 216; Mahon, 112, 137.

[88] Bulow Plantation, sugar plantation south of St. Augustine owned by John Joachim Bulow, destroyed by the Seminole Indians (Jan. 1836). The Bulow Plantation Ruins is now a historic state park at Flagler Beach; Motte, 278-279n7.

[89] Emerich (Emmerich) de Vattel (1714-1767), Swiss philosopher who wrote on international law, published *The Law of Nations* (1758) which applied the theory of natural law to international relations; *Britanica Online Encyclopedia,* http://www.britannica.com/EBchecked/topic/624086/Emmerich-de-Vattel.

[90] Hugo Grotius (1583-1645), Dutch statesman and diplomat, considered the "father of international law" with his works *On the Law of War and*

Peace (1625); *Britanica Online Encyclopedia,*
http://www.britannica.com/search?query=Hugo+Grotius.

[91] Brig. Gen. Abraham (Abram) Eustis, bvt. Brig. Gen. (June 1834) and Col., 1st Arty. (Nov. 1834), acting Florida commanding officer, commanded left wing during Maj. Gen. Scott's campaign; Sprague, 106, 125-126; Heitman, 408.

[92] Maj. Edmund Kirby, Maj. paymaster (1824), special commendation for efficient service during FL campaign (1837), bvt. Lt. Col. and Col. during Mexican War (1847) for gallantry in battles of Contreras, Churubusco, and Chapultepec; Sprague, 173; Heitman, 603.

[93] Maj. Joseph Beard, employed in QM Dept. at Hawkinsville, GA on the Ockmulgee where supplies of rifles and accoutrements were to be supplied for the Creek Campaign; Homans, *A&NC* 4 (23 March 1837), 186, 190.

[94] Capt./Commodore Alexander J. Dallas, USN, commanding officer of West Indies Squadron which included the Caribbean, Gulf of Mexico, and Florida; Mahon, 121, 171; George E. Buker, *Swamp Sailors in the Second Seminole War,* (Gainesville: University Press of Florida, 1997), 47-48.

[95] Capt./Commodore William C. Bolton, USN, commander of the navy yard at Pensacola; Buker, 19.

[96] Capt./Master Commandant Thomas T. Webb, USN, commanding officer of the sloop-of-war *Vandalia*; Buker, 17-19.

[97] Lt. Col. David Emanuel Twiggs, 2nd Dragoons (1836), Brig. Gen. (1846), bvt. Maj. Gen. (1846) for gallantry in several conflicts at Monterey, Mexico; Heitman, 976.

[98] Maj. Richard Augustus Zantziner, 2nd Arty., War of 1812 veteran, bvt. Maj. for ten years faithful service in one grade (1824); Heitman, 1068.

[99] Lt. John Breckinridge Grayson, graduated MA (1826), 1st Lt., 2nd Arty. (1834), Capt. (1838-1846), Capt. C S (1838), bvt. Maj. (1847) for gallantry in Mexican War in battles at Contreras, Churubusco, and Chapultepec, Maj. C S (1852), Brig. Gen. C S A War (1861-1865); Heitman, 479; Cullum, 376.

[100] Lt. Samuel Mackenzie, graduated MA (1818), 1st Lt. 2nd Art. 1825, Capt. 1837; Heitman, 672.

[101] Lt. John C. Casey, graduated MA (1829), 1st Lt., 2nd Arty. (1835), Capt. (1842), 3rd Inf. (1844), chief commissariat (1847-1848) in Mexican War, commissary duty at Tampa Bay (1848-1849), Seminole Indian Emigration Agent (1849-1856); Heitman, 289; Cullum, 426-427.

[102] Lt. George Mitchell Legate, graduated MA (1835), 2nd Lt., 2nd Arty. (1835), resigned (1836); Heitman, 626; Cullum, 590.

[103] Lt. James McCready Morgan, graduated MA (1835), 2nd Lt., 2nd Arty. (1835), 1st Lt., 2nd Arty. (1837), 1st Lt. Ordnance (1838), Capt. Ordnance (1847); Heitman, 725; Cullum, 795-796.

[104] Lt. Benjamin Alvord, graduated MA (1833), 2nd Lt., 4th Inf. (1835), 1st Lt. (1836), bvt. Capt. for gallantry at Battles of Palo Alto and Resala-de-la-Palma, Texas (1846), Capt., 4th Inf. (1846-1854), bvt. Maj. for gallantry at affairs at Paso de Ovejas, National Bridge, and Cerro Gordo, Mexico, Maj. paymaster (1854), Brig. Gen. U.S. Vols. (1862), bvt. Lt. Col., Col., and Brig. Gen. (1865), paymaster gen. USA with rank of Col. and Brig. Gen. (1872-1876), retired after 45 years of active service (1880); Heitman, 161, Cullum, 553-558.

[105] Dr. Henry Lee Heiskell, Asst. Surgeon (1832), Maj. Surgeon (1838); Heitman, 521.

[106] Dr. John C. Reynolds, Asst. Surgeon (1835), resigned (1838), Surgeon Vols. (1846); Heitman, 825.

[107] Capt. Ethan Allen Hitchcock, graduated MA (1817), Capt., 1st Inf. (1824), Maj., 8th Inf. (1838), Lt. Col., 3rd Inf. (1842), bvt. Col. for gallantry in Battles of Contreras and Churubusco, Mexico (1847), bvt. Brig. Gen. for gallantry in Battle of Molino del Rey (1847), Col., 2nd Inf. (1851), Maj. Gen. U. S. Vols. (1862); Heitman, 532; Cullum, 167-179.

[108] Lt. James Farley Izard, gradiated MA (1828), 1st Lt., 1st Dragoons (1833), died of wounds in action with Seminoles at Camp Izard on the Withlacoochee River (28 Feb. 1836); Heitman, 566; Cullum, 414.

[109] Col. Persifor Frazer Smith, LA Vols. (1836), Brig. Gen. LA Vols. (1846), Col. mounted rifles (1846), bvt. Brig. Gen. for gallantry during conflicts at Monterey, Mexico and Battles of Contreras and Churubusco, Mexico; Brig. Gen. (1856); Heitman, 902.

[110] Lt. Col. Thomas Lawson, LA Vols., Surgeon General USA (1836), bvt. Brig. Gen. for meritorious conduct in Mexican War; Heitman, 619.

[111] Maj. Richard Martin Sands, War of 1812 veteran, bvt. Maj. (1829) for ten years faithful service in one grade; Heitman, 859.

[112] Lt. Col. William Stanhope Foster, War of 1812 veteran, Lt. Col., 4th Inf. (1836), bvt. Col. (1837) for distinguished service in FL particularly in Battle of Okeechobee; Heitman, 432. See also *This Miserable Pride of a Soldier: The Letters and Journals of Col. William S. Foster in the Second Seminole War.* Compiled and Edited by John and Mary Lou Missall (Tampa: University of Tampa Press, 2005).

[113] Capt. Samuel Shannon, bvt. Capt. (1830) for ten years faithful service in one grade, Capt. 1st Inf. (1831); Heitman, 877.

[114] Lt. Col. Ichabod Bennett Crane, Lt. Col., 2nd Arty. (1832), Col., 1st Arty. (1843); Heitman, 335.

[115] Col. William Lindsay, War of 1812 veteran, Col., 2nd Arty. (1832); Heitman, 634.

[116] Lt. James Duncan, graduated MA (1834), 2nd Lt., 2nd Arty. (1834), 1st Lt., 2nd Arty. (1836), Capt. 2nd Arty. (1846-1849), bvt. Maj. (1846) for gallantry in Battle of Palo Alto, Texas, bvt. Lt. Col. (1846) for gallantry in

Battle of Resaca-de-la-Palma, Texas, bvt. Col. (1846) for gallantry in Battle of Monterey, Mexico, Col. Inspector Gen. (1849), Heitman, 387; Cullum, 569-570.

[117] Woodburne Potter, the author of this book.

[118] Maj. Mark Anthony Cooper, GA Volunteers. Cooper served in the Georgia House of Representatives and in the U.S. Congress (1839-1843). He was known as the "Iron Man of Georgia" for his iron works near Etowah, GA, which supplied cannon to the Confederacy during the Civil War; *Biographical Directory of the United States Congress.*

[119] John Caesar, Black Seminole leader, killed later in the war (1837); Sprague, 111-113; Kenneth W. Porter, *The Black Seminoles: History of a Freedom-Seeking People.* Rev. and ed. by Alcione M. Amos and Thomas P. Sentry (Gainesville: University Press of Florida, 1996), 74.

[120] Capt. Charles Mynn Thruston, graduated MA (1814), Capt., 3rd Arty. (1827), resigned (1836), Brig. Gen. U. S. vols. (1861); Heitman, 960.

[121] Maj. Gen. Jacob Brown (1775-1828), Commander of forces on the northern frontier during the War of 1812, later Commanding General of the Army; see John D. Morris, *Sword of the Border: Major General Jacob Jennings Brown 1775-1828* (Kent, OH: Kent State University Press, 2000).

[122] Peter Buell Porter (1773-1844), Congressman from New York (1809-1813) & (1815-1816); Major General, New York Militia (1812-1815); New York Secretary of State (1815-1816); U.S. Secretary of War under John Quincy Adams (1828-1829). He was a major supporter of the War of 1812 and served alongside Gaines on the Niagara frontier. *Biographical Directory* http://bioguide.congress.gov/scripts/biodisplay.pl?index=P000446.

[123] Lt. Col. James Bankhead, Lt. Col., 3rd Arty. (1832), Col., 2nd Arty. (1838), bvt. Col. (1838) for meritorious conduct in Florida campaigns, bvt. Brig. Gen. (1847) for meritorious conduct in seige of Veracruz, Mexico; Heitman, 189.

[124] Capt. Clifton Wharton, Capt., 6th Inf. (1830), tr. to 1st Dragoons (1833), Maj. (1836), Lt. Col. (1846); Heitman, 1022.

[125] Euchee (Yuchi, Uchee) Billy, leader of the Uchee band of Indians, was thought killed, but was later killed at Dunlawton Plantation; Mahon, 212.

[126] Maj. William Gates, graduated MA (1806), Maj., 2nd Arty. (1836), Lt. Col., 3rd Arty. (1836), Col., 3rd Arty. (1845), bvt. Brig. Gen. (1865) for long and faithful service in the Army; Heitman, 449; Cullum, 67-68.

[127] Lt. Levin Mynn Powell, U. S. Navy, midshipman (1817), Lt. (1826), penetrated the Everglades in search of Seminoles during the war, commanding officer of brig *Consort* surveying the coast from Apalachicola to the Mississippi River (1840-41), commanded the USS *Potomac* on blockade duty of the Gulf of Mexico during the Civil War (1861-62), appointed rear admiral on retired list (1869); Buker, 21.

Index

Brush, Dr., 118
Bryant, Capt. Thomas (GA Vols.), 129
Bulow Plantation, 118, 119
Bulow, John Joachim., 119
Burial of Dade's Command, 139
Burt, Capt. Alexander (LA Vols.), 134
Butler, Atty. Gen. Benjamin, 38
Butler, Col. P. M. (SC Vols.), 167, 171-173

Caesar, 156, 159
Call, Gen. Richard K., 46, 99, 113, 114
Camden, SC, 127, 129
Camp Blodget, 176
Camp Broadnax, 170, 178
Camp Izard, xi, xii, 148, 156, 167, 175
Camp Misery, 163
Camp Moultrie, 13, 28-30, 49, 56-63, 65, 70
Camp Shelton, 183
Camp Smith, 164, 174
Camp Twiggs, 174
Canadian River, 90
Canfield, Capt., 183
Cantonment Brook. See Fort Brooke
Cape Florida, 117
Capicha Hajo, 20, 21
Capron, Lt., 116
Casey, Lt. John, 133
Cass, Sec. of War Lewis, 27, 37, 85, 194
Catsha Tustenuggee (Little Cloud), 9, 30, 194

cattle, 4, 5, 14, 17, 18, 24, 52, 55, 59, 94, 96, 118, 162, 169, 178, 182
Chamberlain (soldier), 157, 158
Chandler, Lt. Walter, 107
Char Char Tosnusk, 9, 194
Charleston, SC, 25, 124
Charley Amathla, 10, 30, 57, 60, 63, 67, 81, 88, 94, 96-98, 109
Charley Fixico, 178
Charlotte Harbour, 180
Cherokee Indians, 57, 64
Chestnut, Col. (SC Vols.), 127
Cheti Haiola, 9, 88, 194
Chetucksta, 10
Chickasaw Indians, 64
Chicuchatty [Chocachatti], 10, 167-170, 178
Childers, Col. (AL Vols.), 183
Chilly McIntosh, 42
Choctaw Indians, 64
Chokikee, 20, 21, 22
Clark (Clarke), Pvt. Ransom, 107
Clinch, Brig. Gen. Duncan L., 5, 43, 71, 73, 81, 82, 87, 91, 97-99, 101, 102, 109, 111-115, 123, 124, 127, 129, 131, 132, 140-143, 145, 148, 149, 151, 154, 155, 157, 162-167, 174, 181, 182, 194
Clonoto Lassa Creek [Thonotosassa], 183
Coa Hajo, 9, 11, 30, 68, 81, 84, 88, 156, 194

Cochattee Fixico, 88
Conchattee, 10, 89
Congress, United States, 120
Conhatkee Mico, 10, 88, 94, 95
Cooley family, 116, 117
Cooper, Maj. James (FL Vols.), 113, 115, 116
Cooper, Maj. Mark A. (GA Vols.), 151, 167, 178, 181, 182
Cosa Tustenuggee, 9, 89, 194
Cosatchee Amathla, 10, 89
Crane, Lt. Col. Ichabod, 141
Creek Indians, 8, 13, 29, 30, 32, 41-45, 48, 50, 52, 55, 64, 67, 77, 79, 85, 87, 89-92, 146, 184
Cudjoe, 29
Culekeechowa, 25
Cunningham, Capt. S. W. (SC Vols.), 126
Cureton, Capt. John (GA Vols.), 130
Cuthbert, Lt. John, 116

Dade, Maj. Francis L., xii, 102, 103-105, 108, 109, 114, 123, 127, 130, 137-139, 179, 194
Dallas, Comm. Alexander (US Navy), 131, 168
Dalton, Pvt. Kinsley, 87
Dancy, Lt. Francis, 112, 129
Daniels, (unknown), 24
Darien, GA, 124
David Brown (Steamboat), 132
Deamond's Pond, 20
Depeyster, (unknown), 118

Dexter, (unknown), 25
Douglass, Maj. John (GA Vols.), 16, 167, 174
Drane, Capt. Gustavus, 6, 116
Dummett, (unknown), 118
Dunham, (unknown), 119
Dunlawton Plantation, 118
Dupont, (unknown), 119
Duval, Gov. William P., 2, 15, 70

Eaton, Gov. John, 35, 37, 44, 71
Echu Matta, 9, 194
Econchatta Mico, 15
Ellsworth, H. L., 83
Emachitochustern (John Walker), 16
Emathlochee, 10, 88, 194
Enehah, 30
Essayons (Steamboat), 183
Euchee Billy, 171
Eustis, Brig. Gen. Abraham, 124, 125, 167, 171-173, 179, 183
Everett, (unknown), 48

Fanning, Maj. Alex-ander, 112, 113, 115
Finley, Capt. J. E. B. (FL Vols.), 126
Florida, xi, xiii, 1-8, 32, 35, 65, 72, 120, 121, 124, 130, 131, 134, 135, 140, 141, 158, 165, 166
Florida agriculture, 5
Florida Rangers, 167
Florida Volunteers, 116, 162
Floyd, (unknown), 25, 129
Forrester, A., 117

Hamburgh Volunteers (SC
  Vols.), 126
Hamilton, Brig. Gen (SC
  Vols., 125
Hamilton, Dr., 116
Hancock Blues (GA Vols.),
  130
Hancock Troop, 176
Harrall, Dr., 156, 157
Harris, Lt. J. W., 71, 84, 91
Hatch, (unknown), 118
Hathow Matta, 9, 194
Heiskell, Dr. Henry, 133
Henderson, Lt. Richard, 105,
  108
Henry, Capt. George (SC
  Vols.), 171
Heriot, (unknown), 118
Hernandez, Brig. Gen.
  Joseph, 99, 119, 129
Herring, (unknown), 119
Hibler, Capt. Thomas (SC
  Vols.), 171
Hillsboro (Tampa) Bay, 132
Hillsborough (Hillsboro)
  River, 95, 98, 103, 133,
  137, 169, 178, 180, 182
Hitchcock, Capt. Ethan A.,
  134, 146, 157, 158, 160-
  163
Hitchiti Mico, 9, 30, 102, 194
Hitchitipusy, 10
Hithlomee, 20, 21, 22
Hogan, (unknown), 101
Holata Amathla, 10, 30, 53-
  55, 57, 68, 69, 88, 89, 94-
  96, 101
Holata Mico, 9, 11, 30, 56,
  60, 61, 81, 84, 96, 158, 194
House of Representatives, xiv

Humphreys, Gad, 24, 25
Hunter, Lt., 116
Indian population, 2

Izard, Lt. James F., 134, 135,
  144-146, 194

Jackson, President Andrew,
  xiii, 8, 13, 24, 27, 28, 36,
  46-52, 55, 61, 63, 64, 66,
  71, 75, 78, 84, 85, 87, 89,
  90, 92, 194
Jacksonville, 125, 126, 128
Jefferson Cavalry (GA Vols.),
  181, 182
Jesup, Maj. Gen. Thomas,
  xiv, 140, 194
Johnson, Lt., 183
Jumper, 9, 11, 30, 54-57, 60,
  62, 63, 78, 81, 82, 84, 109,
  156-161, 194

Kanapaha Pond (Prairie), 20,
  21
Keayes [Keais], Lt. John,
  105, 108
Ker [Kerr], Capt. Croghan
  (LA Vols.), 134, 145
Kirby, Maj. Edmund, 126,
  167, 171
Kitzler, , 110, 111
Koski Uka, 9, 194

Lake Eustis, 172
Lake George, 3, 100
Lake Monroe, 184
Lake Ponchartrain
  [Pontchartrain], 132
Lang Syne Plantation, 109

201

Lawson, Lt. Col. (Dr.)
  Thomas, 134, 136
Lecotichee, 20
Lee, Capt. J. G. (LA Vols.),
  134
Legate, Lt. George, 133
Legislative Council of
  Florida, 24, 25, 44, 73
Lendrum, Capt. Thomas, 109,
  110, 175
Leon County, 101
Lewis, K. (Creek Indian), 42,
  194
Lindsay, Col. William, 142,
  167, 169, 170, 178, 179,
  181-183
Long Swamp, 9, 20, 21, 93,
  97
Louisiana, 130-133
Louisiana Volunteers, 134,
  136, 145, 146, 148, 156,
  162, 164-168, 174, 176,
  180
Lytle, Maj. J. S., 116

Macon Volunteers (GA
  Vols.), 130
Madison, President James,
  165
Magee, Capt. William (LA
  Vols.), 134
Maitland, Lt. William, 116
Malone, Capt. C. J. (GA
  Vols.), 130, 176, 181
Marks, Capt. H. S. (LA
  Vols.), 134, 156, 168, 169
Marks, Major Samuel (LA
  Vols.), 134, 136
McIntosh, Col. (FL Vols.),
  116

McKenzie, Lt. Samuel, 133
McLemore, Dr. John, 100,
  162, 167, 184
Mellon, Capt. Charles, 116
Merchant (Steamboat), 132
Meriwether, Capt. J. A.
  (GA.Vols.), 130
Miconopy [Micanopy]
  (chief), 9, 11, 26, 28, 30,
  56, 60-62, 66, 68, 81, 82,
  84, 101, 102, 109, 159-161,
  163
Miconopy [Micanopy]
  (town), 100
Micosukee [Miccosukee]
  Indians, 8, 11-12, 19, 93
Mills, Col. William, 115
Minatti, 10
Mississippi River, 28, 29, 31,
  32, 51, 54, 56, 60, 64, 78,
  79, 91
Mobile, AL, 16, 107, 132,
  165, 166
Moke Is She Larni, 9, 30, 81,
  194
Monroe Musqueteers (GA
  Vols.), 130
Monroe, President James, 35
Morgan Guards (GA Vols.),
  130
Morgan, Lt. James, 133
Moultrie Creek, Treaty of,
  See Camp Moultrie
Mountfort, Maj. John, 106,
  107, 133
Mudge, Lt. Robert, 105, 108
Muscogee. See Creek Indians
Musquito Inlet, 171

Negro town, 9

202

Thomas, Pvt. John, 107, 194
Thompson, Wiley, xiii, 18, 22, 25, 57, 62, 65-67, 70, 72-76, 78, 80-83, 85, 86, 90-92, 109-111, 194
Thruston, Capt. Charles, 162
Timrod, Capt. W. H. (SC Vols.), 126
Tokosa Amathla (John Hicks), 30, 62, 63, 88
Tokosa Fixico, 89
Tomoka Creek, 119
Topalargee, 9, 194
Tustenuggee, 10
Tustenuggee Hajo, 88
Tustinuc Hajo, 9, 194
Tustinuc Yaha, 10, 88, 194
Twiggs, Lt. Col. David, 132-134, 154, 157, 164, 165

United States, 1, 14, 25, 29, 30, 38, 41, 42, 46, 49, 51, 52, 61, 65, 67, 68, 76, 77, 79, 83, 129-131, 133, 147, 158

Vattel, Emerich de, 121
Volusia, FL, 126, 167, 168, 171, 172, 183

Wacahouta, FL, 100
Wacooche Hajo, 20-21
Wahoo Swamp, 9, 10, 108
Walker, Capt. (unknown, militia), 16, 18, 19, 22, 23, 87
War Department, xiii, 72, 128, 133, 134

Warren, Col. John, 100, 113, 115, 116
Washington Cavalry (GA Vols.), 130, 176, 181
Washington Light Infantry (SC Vols.), 126
Washington Volunteers (SC Vols.), 126
Watchman (Steamboat), 132
We Flocco Matta, 9, 194
Webb, Capt. (US Navy), 131
Wehalitkee, 20, 22
We-ha-sit-kee, 20
Weightman, Dr. Richard, 116
Wellford, Maj. (FL Vols.), 115
Wharton, Capt. Clifton, 167
White, Joseph, 4, 13, 165, 194
Wilburn, (unknown), 15
Williams, Capt. J. W. (LA Vols.), 134
Williams, Samuel, 119
Williams, W. W., 47
Winslet, (unknown), 48
Withlacochee River. *See* Ouithlacoochee
Witumky, 10, 100

Yaha Amathla, 10, 30, 89
Yaha Fixico, 10, 88, 194
Yaha Hajo, 9, 30, 173, 194
Youman [Yoeman], Lt. John, 116

Zantzinger, Maj. Richard, 133, 176

Made in United States
Orlando, FL
25 February 2025

58899250R00142